Wishing you the best
of everything in the
coming year

Jeanne and John Blocker

Christmas — 75

A Cooking Legacy

A
Cooking Legacy

VIRGINIA T. ELVERSON
MARY ANN McLANAHAN

illustrated by
BETTY T. DUSON

Walker and Company

NEW YORK

First published in the United States of America in 1975 by the WALKER PUBLISHING COMPANY, INC.

Published simultaneously in Canada by FITZHENRY & WHITESIDE LIMITED, TORONTO.

ISBN: 0-8027-0511-7

Library of Congress Catalog Card Number: 75-17479

PRINTED IN THE UNITED STATES OF AMERICA.

Chapter opening illustrations

Page 1, IRON KETTLE; *page 3*, AMERICAN IRON CORN DRYER; *page 14*, HOE BLADE (FOR HOE CAKES); *page 24*, PAUL REVERE SILVER PORRINGER, 1795; *page 79*, NORTH CAROLINA SILVER SUGAR TONGS, SELPH & PYLE, 1780; *page 113*, AMELUNG CASE BOTTLES FOR SPIRITS, 1788; *page 129*, PAUL REVERE SILVER LADLE, 1795.

DESIGNED BY BETTY BINNS

10   9   8   7   6   5   4   3   2   1   0

$\mathcal{A}$CKNOWLEDGEMENTS

A cookbook such as *A Cooking Legacy* is totally dependent upon the interest and generosity of the authors' families and friends, for the rare, unpublished family journals which are quoted throughout the book; for the delicious recipes handed down from generation to generation in treasured notebooks; for the private, priceless decorative art collections which illustrate our text; for the endless hours which went into testing and tasting each recipe. For these and many other gracious gifts of time and effort we are indebted to:

Miss Ima Hogg, who inspired the three of us with her love of Americana; Mrs. Joseph G. Thompson, who played "put and take" until our recipes pleased even her gourmet tastes; Mrs. Clare T. Spangler, Administrative Assistant at The Museum of Fine Arts, Houston, who typed our manuscript with never a complaint over changes and rewrites; Mrs. William C. Touret, Mrs. Justin S. Morrill, Mrs. Arthur D. Dyess, Jr., and Mrs. Douglas S. Craig, each of whom shared with us her own unique family journals and recipes. These heretofore unpublished insights into the early Colonial life of Rhode Island, Pennsylvania and New York, and the nineteenth-century customs of the plantation owner's South, added a richness and depth to our text which was not duplicated in many published sources which we studied.

To the following friends who gave of their professional counsel or their culinary expertise, we are deeply grateful: Mr. David B. Warren, Associate Director, The Museum of Fine Arts, Houston; Mr. Barry Green-law, Curator, The Bayou Bend Collection; Mr. Lonn Taylor, Curator, Winedale Restoration; Mr. O. B. Dyer, Interior Supervisor, The Bayou Bend Collection; Mrs. Helen Duprey Bullock, formerly of the National Trust for Historic Preservation; Mrs. Gail C. Belden, Assistant Curator, Winterthur; Mr. Paul H. Harris, formerly of the Henry Ford Museum; Mr. John A. Castellani, Librarian, Mount Vernon, Virginia; special thanks to L. Proctor Thomas for his helpful legal advice; Mr. Wendell Garrett, Editor and publisher of *The Magazine* ANTIQUES.

And to Mrs. John Mawhinney, Mrs. Raymond Risien, Mrs. William Broyles, Mrs. T. Allen Bynum, Mrs. Teckler Borgstedt, Mrs. Flora Jahnz, Mrs. Stanley Shipnes, Mrs. William T. Mendell, Mrs. Allen H. Carruth, Mrs. James W. Hargrove, Mrs. C. Brien Dillon, Mrs. George R. Brown, Mr. Cleto Hernandez, Mrs. C. P. Duson, Sr., Mrs. Donald Duson, Mrs. Adela Posadas, Mrs. William Wareing, Mrs. Albert M. Tomforde, the Dowager Countess of Radnor, O.B.E., and Mrs. Charles E. Richards, Jr., Mrs. George A. Peterson, Mrs. Thomas G. Tucker, Mrs. James C. Rich-dale, Mrs. M. L. Adams, Mrs. W. L. Edmundson, Mrs. I. C. Kerridge, Mrs. Pat Perini, Mrs. Robert Buckner, Mrs. Wilbur Moore.

Our illustrations are drawings of rare artifacts most graciously shown to us by the following public and private collectors: The Bayou Bend Collection; Winedale Restoration; Henkel Square Restoration; The Anson-Jones House; Varner-Hogg Plantation; Mr. and Mrs. James Britton, Jr.; Mr. and Mrs. Spurgeon K. Britt; Mr. and Mrs. Thomas D. Anderson; Mr. and Mrs. Robin Elverson; Dr. and Mrs. Lynn A. Bernard; Mr. and Mrs. Paul Gervais Bell; Mr. and Mrs. Fred T. Couper, Jr.; Mr. and Mrs. Harris Masterson III; Mr. and Mrs. Robert Jameson; Mr. and Mrs. C. Pharr Duson, Jr., Mr. and Mrs. Robert F. Strange; Mr. and Mrs. Peter G. Brooks; Mrs. Charles L. Bybee; Mrs. Doris Duckworth; Dr. and Mrs. John E. Martin; Mrs. Albert M. Tomforde; Mrs. Hazel Ledbetter; and Mr. and Mrs. George A. Butler.

Lastly, a warm "Thank You" to our families, who patiently tasted their way through these recipes that we might assure you of the culinary pleasures to be found within the pages of *A Cooking Legacy*.

THE AUTHORS

FOREWORD

It has been my great good fortune in life to see a number of my fondest dreams reach fruition. The success of these endeavors has rested very largely upon the loyal and enthusiastic help of many people. The Collection of American Decorative Arts at Bayou Bend is no exception. Begun by my brothers and myself in 1920, it now belongs to The Museum of Fine Arts, Houston, and the interested peoples of the world.

The three friends who have written this cookbook were among those who helped, in the very beginning, to document and study The Bayou Bend Collection, and present it to the public for the first time. They profess to owe much to me for their interest and their knowledge of this exciting period in our country's growth. I am honored by their dedication and feel that I, in turn, owe much to them.

Their talents and their scholarship, as represented in A Cooking Legacy *will take the true flavor of America's illustrious past into many present-day homes, where such culinary pleasures may well have been a treasure heretofore unexplored. I know that each of you will enjoy, as I have, the fascinating facts and delicious recipes gathered in these pages.*

Ima Hogg

Contents

Introduction

Colonial American pioneers left diaries and journals telling tragic stories of the deaths of nine out of every ten early settlers. "Starving time" it was called. The forests teemed with game, large and small; the waters swarmed with fish; fruits and vegetables were plentiful. Unfortunately many of these early Colonials were city-bred and unfamiliar with country living; even those from rural backgrounds were unprepared for wilderness existence. They failed to bring the necessary tools and equipment and knowledge to cope with their new way of life, and so their spiritual diet became one of fear and desperation.

Adaptation was the key to survival. The American Indian became both teacher and savior, instructing the settlers in hunting, food preparation and preservation. Cookbooks from home would have been of little use to the often illiterate housewife, who found herself obliged to prepare ingredients unknown to her in England or Holland, such as corn, pumpkin and squash.

By the late seventeenth century it was clear that America was being dominated by two principal cultural heritages: Northern European, largely Protestant and English, and Iberian, Catholic and Spanish. It is important to remember that Spain began colonization a full century before the Brit-

1

ish and French. France's only lasting culinary influence is found in southern Louisiana.

While the cultural influences of the Protestants—English, Scotch-Irish, Welsh, German and Dutch—were blending, the religious barrier precluded Catholics from partaking in this cross-pollination. A string of Spanish missions from Texas through New Mexico, Arizona and California established a vigorous trade in cereals, wines and beef. Interestingly, these cattle were descended from those brought to Mexico by the Spaniards over 200 years earlier. It is from this strain that the famous Texas Longhorn emerged. Through the Spanish and Indian influences a "Mexican style" of cooking developed, featuring corn, wheat, meat, beans, onions and peppers.

In the late seventeenth century the courageous American Colonists developed eating habits that remained roughly the same for the next hundred years. They prepared and devoured enormous quantities of basically the same foods. Naturally, economic, geographic and ethnic factors created certain differences. When the frontier phase passed, the ecology changed. As settlers killed off the larger game in the forests the smaller game became more plentiful. Gardens expanded and crops were diversified.

We can readily understand the lusty and excessive alcoholic drinking habits of these early Colonists when we visualize their daily plight in facing an unknown, frightening wilderness, with death an unyielding companion. The old-world traditions coupled with lack of sanitary precautions encouraged a considerable consumption of alcoholic drinks by all ages.

An interesting democracy developed as a result of frontier living. The planter and ploughman worked side by side, as did the mistress and her maid. The servant of England became the "help" and often "friend" in the Colonies. In the days of knee breeches and powdered wigs, urban living brought to America a wealthy society and well-informed merchant class. The Southern tobacco planter or the Northern shipping magnate, eager and able to keep up with the Joneses, could produce a banquet that would overwhelm the best-equipped caterer today. Styles and tastes were affected by increased travel and the few European and English publications which found their way to the New World. The road to prosperity and prestige had once been through the Church. In Colonial America, however, it was through the countinghouses of the merchants. These Colonials were fiercely proud of their ability to succeed in the face of hardship. These daring men, full of audacity, paved the way for the nineteenth-century industrialists whose creed, "nothing ventured—nothing gained," served them well.

An adventure in good eating, spiced with a bit of social history, awaits the reader who will follow these pages back in time and thus taste a bit of Colonial America.

The Way It Was

Research on Early American eating and drinking habits is both fascinating and frustrating. The early "receipts" (pronounced re-ceets) were more what we would call guidelines today. They were in no way detailed instructions. Finding a new undiscovered recipe is almost an impossibility, for what was good long ago has survived in a fairly recognizable form to this day. The eighteenth-century egg and bacon pie is today's *quiche lorraine*. The purpose of this book is to entertain the reader with highlights of American culinary heritage and to provide a collection of recipes, adapted from early sources, which are both delicious and practical. Included are variations devised by the authors as they tested. These recipes are, in a sense, all original because they are the result of personal adaptations from old recipes and are not based upon known modern recipes. The reader will discover delicious results from "new" combinations of herbs, spices, meats and vegetables, as well as new tastes in breads and desserts.

Adapting eighteenth- and nineteenth-century recipes is an exciting adventure. Guidelines calling for "a wine glass of . . . ," "two porringers of . . . ," "as much mace as needed," "boil at 2 or 3 wollops," all add to the confusion of translating these delights into workable twentieth-century

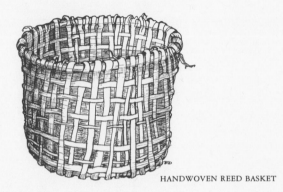

HANDWOVEN REED BASKET

reality. These early receipts provided an exciting jumping-off place. After they were adapted, each was tested by three different cooks in three different kitchens. Many problems involving measurements of ingredients such as flour and sugar had to be solved. The coarse sugar of the seventeenth century bears little resemblance to today's refined product. A cake described in an eighteenth-century American housewife's diary called for ten to twelve eggs. Those quail-sized eggs produced by the scrawny chickens surviving on the fringes of a wilderness were quite different from today's mass-produced, graded variety.

What were the sources of early American receipts? There were basically two main derivations, English cookbooks and Indian methods. The development of cookbook styles is interesting to trace. They were quite different in makeup centuries ago. The fifteenth- and sixteenth-century cookbooks were more concerned with instructions involving the placement of food on the table, serving methods and table manners, than in recipes. A popular English cookbook printed in 1665, *The Queen's Closet Opened. Incomparable Secrets in Physick, Chirurgery, Preserving, Candying and Cooking*, seems to have included everything the housewife would ever need to know. Another in 1660, *The Accomplisht Cook Approved by the Fifty Years Experience and Industry of Robert May in his Attendance on Several Persons of Honour*, provided fascinating reading. An Englishman, Dr. Trusler, printed in 1788 *The Honours of the Table*, which forms a bridge between the early form of cookbooks and the familiar versions of today. The last great book of this early tradition was Mrs. Beeton's *Book of Household Management* published in hard cover in 1861. Non-American eighteenth-century cookbooks began the trend toward recipe books enriched with international flavor and customs.

The first truly American cookbook, *American Cooking*, was printed in the Colonies in 1796. Its author, Amelia Simmons, had the book printed at her own expense. She had been unable to find anyone willing to publish it. Thus appeared the first recipes for pumpkin pudding, crooknecked squash, ashcakes, slapjacks and Indian pudding—American dishes, all!

Early American housewives kept notebooks of their recipes, medicinal concoctions and cleaning secrets. These were handed down for generations. Several recipes in this book are derived from unpublished early notebooks. They are difficult to translate because standard forms of measurement were not adopted until the nineteenth century. While American housewives were writing successful cookbooks, other countries left this task to professionals, usually men, until the nineteenth century. Colonial America did not attract professional cooks from other lands. The few who did immigrate zealously guarded their secrets. In Colonial cities cooking schools sprang up to instruct fashionable young women in the "art of cooking and making of desserts." As hotels and restaurants multiplied in America, chefs were brought from France, Switzerland, Germany and Italy. They certainly added a great deal to the American melting pot of culinary art.

How very grateful was the early settler for corn! Necessity, the mother of invention, provided countless uses for this wonderful food. The Colonists, faced with too little time to accomplish what they must, were delighted with the simple cultivation the crop required. Corn grew in all climates and could be planted between trees and stumps, unlike the imported wheat and rye which were difficult to sow and reap. The settlers quickly grew accustomed to the strangely bitter and nutty flavor of their new staple. The corn we eat today is a development of the strain grown by an Indian tribe in upstate New York, which was discovered by the settlers near the end of the Colonial period. By 1619 a Jamestown harvest was large enough to permit rent payment in barrels of corn. Interestingly, corn was never served as a vegetable. It was turned into cornmeal and then translated into porridge, hominy, succotash, mush, Indian pudding, breads, and even a tenuous cheese. As time went on the South grew to prefer white cornmeal while the North preferred the yellow. Popcorn delighted all ages then as now. Bread made from cornmeal alone dried out too quickly and so the Colonists devised "rye'n'Injun" bread which was corn and rye meal mixed. The "Colonial corn" was more starchy and tough

EARLY SALT GLAZE JUG
WITH CORNCOB STOPPER

and ripened in many colors. Each tribe usually dried its own color of corn. At husking bees a man finding a red ear of corn was granted a kiss from the girl of his choice. This custom was copied from a more shocking Indian version. Jugs of corn whiskey, and other jugs and bottles, had stoppers of corncobs. Cob slices were used as knife handles, bowls for pipes, checkerboard men and smoking fuel. No part of the crop was wasted—husks were used to stuff mattresses, fashion chair seats, and even to furnish a form of toilet tissue!

The potato became a Colonial staple by the second half of the eighteenth century. The earliest settlers ate them only out of necessity for they thought their taste too bland, and there were stories that they were poisonous, perhaps due to the fact that they are not mentioned in the Bible. The warm climate yams, however, enjoyed great popularity, as did the Bermuda sweet onion.

Of prime interest to the early settler were his apple trees. There were many varieties planted, some suited best for cider, others for sauces, dumplings, Dutch apple butter and the like. The English apple tart became American apple pie. With apple crops flourishing, cider soon replaced beer in popularity. One Yankee village of forty families produced 3,000 barrels of cider in the year 1721. No doubt much of it was sold; but, as Horace Greeley was to estimate a bit later, in the early 1800s the average New Hampshire family of six or eight would easily consume one barrel of cider a week. Often a man's worth was determined by his private store of this beverage. Actually the hard-working and hard-drinking pioneers invented ingenious ways of fermenting all sorts of roots and shrubs.

Beer was believed to have medicinal qualities that could prevent scurvy. All economic levels enjoyed its hearty flavor. Students at Harvard College paid a portion of their tuition in wheat and malt. These supplied the brewhouse maintained by the school. Beers were rated as strong, middling

IRON TRIVET RACK
AND WARMING TRIVETS

AMERICAN CURVED-
IRON MEAT FORK

and small, depending on the alcoholic content and brewing techniques. Stronger drinks such as ale and porter, combining three types of malts, were eighteenth-century inventions and largely imported.

By 1670 imported and domestic whiskeys were rivaling rum in popularity. Though wild grapes were plentiful, wine making did not seem to interest the Colonists. Perhaps Colonial America's greatest contributions to the art of drinking came in the form of corn whiskey and the mixed-drink appetizers. It was not until much later that the Temperance movement clouded men's minds with feelings of guilt over the sinfulness of drink.

The earliest settlements were arrival and departure points, and there the first cities developed. Americans had little desire then to be tucked away in isolated seclusion, as they do today. We can easily picture the hard life of the Colonial men clearing the wilderness with their felling axes or hunting in their heavy leather breeches, carrying musket and sword in hand. The arduous discipline demanded of the women is harder to appreciate and much less romantic. Aside from the normal household chores, a woman provided her family with all of its clothes and linens. She served as family doctor. It was important that she be able to handle a gun in case of Indian or animal attack. Learning to prepare the foods which nature provided and reproducing old favorites with the unsophisticated tools at her disposal was a full-time job. To this was added the necessity of preserving cooked game, vegetables and fruits for the seasons ahead. A few of the native vegetables available were okra, lima and kidney beans, black-eyed peas, yams, pumpkins and cranberries. Rice came to America in the late 1600s, as stories tell, when a ship, blown off course, landed for repairs in Charleston, South Carolina. The ship's captain, having sailed all the way from Madagascar, out of gratitude gave a handful of rice grains to the governor. There is mention, however, in early journals, of wild rice in the New England Colonies.

Domestic animals such as cattle, hogs, goats, chickens, geese and sheep were plentiful by the mid-1600s. Mutton was never as plentiful in the Colonies as it had been in England, for sheep were impractical to raise among the wild briars of the landscape. Venison and turkey dishes were common mealtime fare. The shorelines provided such game as plover, crane, snipe, duck and goose. Inland were lark and pigeon; many varieties such as the passenger pigeon and heath hen became extinct due to excessive hunting.

Fish presented a problem for some of the new Americans. Many early settlers were not knowledgeable fishermen, and they found preparing and consuming the unknown species of fish quite unappetizing. They were thus ill-prepared to take advantage of the bountiful foods available in the waters of their new home. Again necessity saw to it that the Colonists overcame their fears. Soon iron kettles filled with water and vinegar contained simmering sturgeon, salmon and skate. Smaller fish were roasted and fried or preserved by salting or smoking; among these were perch, flounder, pike, mullet, haddock, catfish, bass and alewives. Oysters and oyster dishes were eaten plain and embellished, and the shells were used for binding mortar and building roads.

For the earliest settlers, fish that could be gathered easily along the coastline became a mainstay in their diet. One-dish fish meals such as clam chowder or oyster stew were common in New England then as now. Planked shad is another dish brought down through the years. Maryland invented succulent crab cakes. The gentry of New York enjoyed barbecuing a turtle once or twice a week. All along the coastline shellfish and frogs became popular "made" or "regular" dishes. Early cookbooks define "made" dishes as those requiring a number of ingredients as opposed to "regular" dishes, which were roasted, fried or boiled.

The air sacs and swimming bladders of fish became specialties. In the South alligator meat was thought to cure cancer and ulcers. Turtle eggs were thought to stimulate men's virility. Another dish eaten by New England fishermen for sexual vitality was boiled whale's testicles. The sailors believed this organ of the whale prolonged their youth and vigor. Colonial stories relate descriptions of these "youthful" sailors returning home from a year or two at sea to find their women aged and haggard in appearance, while the husbands had remained healthy and fit!

Imported necessities were sugar from the West Indies, spices from the Far East by way of England, and molasses from Barbados. Imported luxuries were English beer and tea, European wines, oranges and lemons, coffee and chocolate. Food to be preserved was often salted. Since native salt was too low in saline, "Bay of Biscay" salt had to be imported for this purpose. Another variety, "Liverpool" salt, was imported for table use.

Colonists often followed the Indian method of preserving meat, called "jerking," by drying thin strips of meat in the sun. Later colonists enhanced the flavor by drying the meat in smokehouses. If kept dry this jerky lasted almost indefinitely. Pickling was more expensive than salting,

AMERICAN IRON
STEW KETTLE

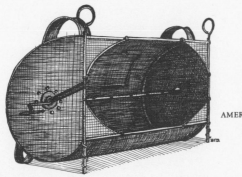

AMERICAN TIN BIRD ROASTER

but this was the method most frequently used for vegetables. Oysters, which were a great favorite for late supper, were one of the foods which had to be cooked before pickling. Pigs' feet were soaked in brine, pickled and stored in spiced vinegar. Stone or glass jars were used because vinegar could not penetrate them. "Sousing" was a method of fancy pickling.

Cooked foods were also "potted"—packed tightly, forced into earthen-ware pots, and sealed with clarified butter. Sausage is a form of potted food; the meat is forced tightly into a container, in this case a skin.

Many fruits and vegetables were dried in the sun, Indian fashion. Sweetmeats were preserved in sugar. Fruits were put up then much as they are today.

In the South little boxhouses were built over cool springs to store food. Underground rooms or even holes served as icehouses. The ice was shipped from the North, packed in straw or sawdust, then wrapped in strips of flannel and held in place between slabs of stone. In the North food was often frozen in the snow. In the Middle Colonies, Dutch cellars were holes dug out of hillsides. Large homes had brick-lined pits. Buckets were hung down wells everywhere in the Colonies. Here would hang a frothy sylla-bub or flummery for a special dessert.

By the late eighteenth century cellars were well stocked with dried beef and pork, cider, potatoes, turnips, beets, carrots and cabbage. Some vegeta-bles were buried in sand, covered with layers of straw, and topped with salt. There were heavily scented bunches of herbs suspended from the rafters above, and strings of apples, onions, peaches and pumpkins hanging from pegs.

We know that food in Colonial times was certainly plentiful and whole-some but just how it tasted is somewhat a matter for conjecture. Most cooking was done in large iron pots; in the fireplace the pots were sus-pended over the fire or raised above the embers by means of little legs. Lug poles of wood or iron were built into the fireplace wall, providing a rack on which to suspend the cooking pots. These poles were later replaced by a more practical swinging crane. The distance from the fire was adjust-

WOODEN TRENCHER
AND SPOON, 1760

ed by S-shaped hooks, adjustable trammels and chains. Though utensils had long handles, the cook in her long full skirt had to be extremely careful to avoid live coals and spitting grease. The floor was swept constantly and scrubbed around the hearth to prevent the house catching fire.

Stewing, slow boiling and roasting seem to have been the most common methods of cooking, for animals were not slaughtered until they had outlived all other usefulness. A dish that contained both meat and vegetables (made dish) was ideal because of the ease of preparation. Stews, boiled dinners, porridges and gruels were undoubtedly the daily fare. There was relatively little frying because of the danger posed by the open fire.

The earliest roasting was done on spits turned by hand, usually by the children of the family. Andirons were equipped with a series of notches for supporting the spit upon which the meat was skewered. A pan was placed on the hearth below to catch the drippings. The eighteenth century produced clock-driven jacks with weights and pulleys. One unusual innovation employed a dog, trained to walk a treadmill which turned a complex system of wheels connected to a spit. Smokejacks (a fifteenth-century invention by Leonardo da Vinci) resembling small windmills were turned by the updrafts from the fire. Late in the seventeenth century a metal box, with its own spit, was developed to cook tender cuts or game.

Since meats and vegetables were prepared simply, the more elaborate kitchen tools found in early Colonial kitchens were for the preparation of desserts. In most kitchens one would have found pie crimpers, to press together the edges of the pies; pastry jiggers, to give decorative edges to cookies; wooden or pierced-tin sieves, for berries and nuts; elaborate molds

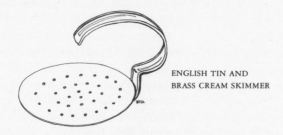

ENGLISH TIN AND
BRASS CREAM SKIMMER

for jellies; and egg beaters of various descriptions. Utensils were made of wood, iron or bellmetal. Brass and copper became more popular when they were introduced through the seaports along the coastline. Tin implements were usually made of heavy sheet iron plated with tin. All fully equipped kitchens had stoneware crocks, pitchers, basins and molds.

In the eighteenth century as the Colonies prospered and great personal fortunes were made, many women in the North as well as the South left food preparation and cleaning-up chores to slaves or other kitchen help. The mistress delighted, however, in assisting in the preparation of special dainty desserts for balls or feasts. Colonists welcomed any excuse to prepare such a special meal. Sunday dinner in the South generally was treated as though it were a special banquet. Then there were christenings, funerals, church days, birthdays of all kinds, fox hunts, horse races and weddings. Often two occasions overlapped, providing further excuse for gastronomic splendor. Sugaring-off feasts in the spring were popular in New

MILKING STOOL

England. Journals tell of wealthy parents leaving home for a day and allowing their children, overseen by a trusted servant, to entertain their friends.

In the South, kitchens were generally separated from the main house, and food was carried into the house and reheated in special hot-water dishes and chafing dishes. In Northern mansions, kitchens were often located in the basements. There, too, the reheating of foods was necessary.

As would be expected, table settings were simple and crude in the seventeenth century. A bare board on trestles served as a table around which the family stood; our expression "room and board" comes from this early form of dining table. If the family owned a chair, the father sat! Joint stools soon were available for the rest of the family. Standing or sitting, the children maintained strict silence during meals. Plates and spoons were of wooden treenware or of pewter. Plates, called trenchers, were simply flat pieces of wood with shallow indentations carved on each side. The depressions kept gravies and sauces from spilling out. Often two shared a trencher and when courting couples were seen sharing one trencher it was assumed they were engaged. It has been suggested that the term "trench

11

mouth" derived from this early eating custom.

Many meals were eaten directly from a common pot. The three middle fingers served as a spoon. Bits of bread were sometimes used with these meat stews, which were then called "spoon meat." It is no wonder that all families had large quantities of enormous napkins to be tied around the neck. Since washday came only approximately once a month, it was imperative to have a huge supply of napkins to last from one washday to the next.

By the mideighteenth century, knives and forks were in use. In the beginning forks were two-tined implements used chiefly to hold down meat while it was being cut. Gradually the three-tined fork appeared in steel with a bone or horn handle. Later they were made of silver. Since knives were then no longer needed to spear food, they became rounded on the ends and soon were being made in silver to match the forks. These utensils were highly valued and were prized as important gifts. Guests invited for dinner often brought their own tableware as few households were equipped to supply visitors with eating utensils. Perhaps for this reason the "sucket spoon" was developed. This was a clever utensil with a spoon on one end and a fork on the other, a convenient traveling device. After meals, used dishes were carried from the table in large baskets called voiders. Little dishwashing was done in the home because of the difficulty of transporting water. Trenchers were probably wiped and put away until the next meal. Cooking pots were transported downstream for washing; this had to be done to protect the drinking water.

Until about 1800, when French customs became influential, all dishes, even in the wealthiest homes, were placed on the table to be passed from one person to the other. One French custom called for the lady to serve the soup, salad and dessert, and for the host to serve the rest. By 1850, the *à la russe* system of having servants pass all dishes became the custom. During the period when dishes were placed on the table, cookbooks diagrammed elaborate ways to arrange each dish, balancing it with others in a pleasing fashion.

Separate dining rooms appeared in the eighteenth century in cities and in elegant country homes, and so more attention was paid to the art of dining. Chairs were now available for each diner. Most families used tablecloths, except for desserts and after-dessert fruits, nuts and liqueurs. Napkins, it seems, were still tied about the neck. Large standing salts went out of fashion and smaller "trencher" salts were used. Épergnes made their appearance in the middle of the century and were adorned with fruits, sweetmeats and occasionally flowers. Silver candelabra were placed on the table only when needed for light and otherwise stood on a side table. China plates appeared in wealthy homes, but pewter was still in more general use. Covered dishes were important in order to keep food hot, as were plate-warming racks and baskets. One wineglass was placed at each place

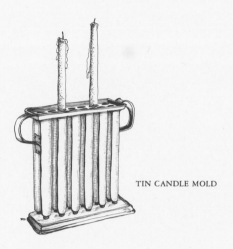

TIN CANDLE MOLD

until late in the century, when more glasses were added. Crystal wine rinsers were on the table so that glasses could be cleansed between wines. Decanters, wine slides (for moving bottles around the table) and wine labels, hung on bottles, became popular. Wine funnels for straining and decanting were used in the care and handling of fine wines. Finger bowls were used for rinsing the mouth as well as the fingers. Some records hint that bubbling and blowing noises were often heard behind napkins held as curtains hiding the diner and his finger bowl. The table of the late 1800s was as finely dressed as those patriotic zealots who sat about it raising their glasses of Madeira and Port in confident toasts to the future of the Republic.

An emerging industrialization brought many changes to foods and eating habits. Various methods of preserving foods were introduced. Some methods of adulterating foods began to cause the government concern as early as the nineteenth century. The principle of refrigeration and the appearance of the tin can revolutionized American cooking habits. By the 1830s, many Europeans, weary of wars and poverty, were attracted to the United States. These Bavarians, Saxons, Austrians, Hungarians, Belgians, Swiss, Dutch and Prussians came in search of a new life, bringing with them new ideas in cooking to season the American melting pot.

Breakfast

The Colonial American breakfast was far from the juice, eggs and bacon of today. The stoic early settlers rose early and went straight to the chores that demanded their attention. In frontier outposts and on farms, families drank cider or beer and gulped down a bowl of porridge that had been cooking slowly all night over the embers. There was no gathering together among the adults for a second cup of coffee and in most homes no sitting at all for breakfast. Customs changed as the country matured and urban living developed.

In the towns, the usual mug of alcoholic beverage consumed upon rising was followed by cornmeal mush and molasses with more cider or beer. By the nineteenth century, breakfast was served as late as 9 and 10 o'clock. Here might be found coffee, tea or chocolate, wafers, muffins, toasts, and a butter dish and knife. The ability to afford sugar was a yardstick measuring the excellence of the tablefare. The southern poor ate cold turkey washed down with the ever-present cider. The size of breakfasts grew in direct proportion to growth in wealth. Breads, cold meats and, especially in the Northeast, fruit pies and pasties joined the breakfast menus. Families in the Middle Colonies added special items such as scrapple (cornmeal and headcheese) and Dutch sweetcakes which were fried in deep fat.

14

It was among the Southern planters that breakfast became a leisurely and delightful meal, though it was not served until early chores were attended to and orders for the day given. The planter most likely downed a mug of cider, ale or beer upon rising and went into the fields to organize the work. He then returned to the house and was joined by his family, and often houseguests, for a lavish breakfast around 9:30. To the coffee, breads, cold meats and fruit pies being consumed by his affluent Northern counterparts, he often added cheese, meat pasties, fresh fruits, eggs on occasion, and the famous Virginia ham. One Colonial gastronome recalls breakfasting on pickled oysters and hot chocolate! Benjamin Franklin, it is said, enjoyed a bowl of porridge with honey and nutmeg, a bit of bread and butter, and tea. In the eighteenth century there was ample room for choice and personal taste at the breakfast table.

Breads were eaten at all times of the day but particularly at breakfast. In the seventeenth century baking was generally done once a week in great quantities. This backbreaking procedure involved both many hours of preparation and the undivided attention of the women. Ovens were small enclosed compartments built right into the chimney next to the open hearth and opening into the fireplace itself or into the room. These openings had doors made of wood or iron. A fire made from special hard "oven" wood was ignited in the oven. When the cook felt the correct amount of heat was being generated for the particular baking to be done, she removed the wood and embers, swept the oven floor clean, and spread a layer of fresh clean leaves, sprinkled with cornmeal to keep the dough from sticking. The loaves were placed inside and the oven tightly sealed. This was all done just before the family retired for the night. What wonderful dreams the pleasant smells must have conjured up, except for the poor housewife who misjudged her oven temperature. Her loaves turned

POTTERY ANT TRAP

out burnt on the outside and doughy inside. As the loaves were removed from the oven (on long-handled wooden paddles called peels), the housewife could see whether or not her loaves needed "rasping," the term for scraping off the crust that had burned. Biscuits, shortbread and pone were baked in "bake-kettles," banked in hot embers in the fireplace. These kettles, with close-fitting lids, were made of heavy iron and stood in the fireplace on three small legs. Cast-iron stoves with ovens were introduced in the nineteenth century. Mrs. Child, in her cookbook, admonishes the housewife: "An hour is long enough to heat an oven for flour bread; pumpkin pies will bear more. If you are afraid your oven is too hot, throw in a little flour and shut it up for a minute. If it scorches black immediately, the heat is too furious; if it merely browns, it is right. Some people wet an old broom two or three times and turn it round near the top of the oven till it dries; this prevents pies and cakes from scorching near the top.''

Corn was used in breads throughout the Colonies, but other wheat substitutes such as potatoes, rice and dried pumpkin were also used. Corn bread, hoecakes (meal and water cooked over the fire on a hoe), and johnnycakes were among the most popular varieties. Ashcakes (cooked in leaves in the ashes), scratchback (made from a thick corn pudding which was uneven on top and scratched the roof of the mouth), fried corn dabs, and beaten biscuits (beaten with an axe handle for at least an hour) were other interesting types of breads the early settlers enjoyed eating.

Leavened breads, or white breads, were considered luxuries and were made only for special occasions. Yeast was scarce and expensive, and so sourdough cultures, potash, pearl ash and beer barrel ''emptins'' were used as leavening agents. How to make pearl ash was discovered in the Colonies in the 1700s, and it was exported in great quantities. Commercial baking powder was produced in Boston in the late 1850s.

Leftover scraps and crusts were always saved and used in puddings, bread sauces, and even in cake ''receipts.'' The modern family probably does not utilize leftover bread scraps enough or realize their potential for use in many different dishes.

Twentieth-century tastes may find Colonial breakfast dishes more palatable at brunch, lunch or supper. Many of the recipes in this book will lead the imaginative cook down new paths of discovery and the reader may delight in finding money-saving recipes containing wholesome and delicious food.

✳❀✳ A Good Mixed Bread

PUT a tea-spoonful of salt, and a large one of yeast, into a quart of flour; make it sufficiently soft, with corn meal gruel; when well risen, bake it in a mould. It is an excellent bread for breakfast. Indifferent flour will rise much better, when made with gruel than with fair water.

The Virginia Housewife: or, Methodical Cook
Mrs. Mary Randolph, 1824

What more delightful aroma can be conjured up than that of a fragrant, yeasty loaf of fresh bread! And what sheer smugness to say, "I made it myself." It's the easiest and most satisfying accomplishment—even a child will have no trouble making delicious crusty bread. This is a good basic recipe.

✳ Crusty Bread

2 packages dried yeast	1 tablespoon vegetable oil
1 tablespoon sugar	5 cups unbleached flour
2 cups warm water (110° to 115°)	2½ teaspoons salt

Mix yeast and sugar and dissolve it in ½ cup of the warm water. Add the oil. Meanwhile, sift the flour and salt 5 times. Make a well in the center and pour in remaining 1½ cups water and the yeast mixture. Mix vigorously. Dough should be soft and sticky, so it may be necessary to add more water; if needed, add 1 tablespoon at a time, carefully, until texture is just right. Let stand for about 10 minutes. Turn out onto a floured board and knead by pushing with the heel of your hand and folding dough over, turning it in quarter circles each time. Sprinkle with additional flour to prevent sticking. When dough begins to feel elastic and springy, form it into a ball and put into a clean dry bowl. Cover with a clean tea towel and let rise at about 75° temperature till double in size, about 1 hour. Remove to a floured board and knead again for 5 to 10 minutes. Return to the bowl, cover, and let rise again till double in bulk. Now, divide dough into 3 parts. Knead each one separately, and shape them into long sausage shapes. Place on a lightly greased cookie sheet that has been sprinkled with cornmeal. Make several diagonal gashes across the top of each loaf. Cover and let rise in a draft-free place till almost triple in size, 1½ to 2 hours. Spray lightly with a fine mist of water. Bake in 375° oven for 20 to 25 minutes, until loaves sound hollow when tapped. Remove and cool on wire rack, or prop each loaf on end.

A FEW SIMPLE RULES AND
FACTS ABOUT BREAD MAKING

1 Flours vary in their ability to absorb liquid; therefore, it is not possible to give an exact amount of water.
2 Stone-ground, unbleached flour makes the best and crustiest breads. Part of the flour amounts given may be substituted with whole-wheat

flour, usually half. Or ½ cup of wheat germ or macroflaked wheat or corn or rye, which has been put through a blender before adding. Experiment with various types of flours.

3 The sugar and oil are not absolutely essential, but they do give the yeast something on which to grow quickly.

4 Bread made with water will have a crisper crust than bread made with milk.

5 Kneading produces a smoother texture. Three kneadings and risings seem to have the best results. One kneading produces a coarser-textured bread with large holes, and a bread that does not rise as easily. If your loaves have the "audacity" to fall (due to a cold draft, etc.) before the baking, simply knead them briefly once again and let them rise. (An old Southern Indiana saying sums up the problem: "It squatted to rise but it baked in a squat.") Bake as usual after the rising. Yeast is a living thing that grows to produce the light texture bread requires.

6 Spraying bread with water before and during baking makes a crisper crust.

7 Bread should rise in a draft-free spot at a constant temperature of about 75°. Slow rising is best.

8 An ideal place for bread to rise is in a cold oven with the door closed. Place a large bowl or pan of hot water on the bottom shelf below the rising dough. If your hot water heater is in a closet in the kitchen, this also makes an admirable spot.

❋ Sally Lunn

1 package dried yeast
¼ cup lukewarm water (110° to
   115°)
2 cups milk
4 tablespoons sugar

1 cup melted shortening
3 eggs
5 cups flour, sifted
1 teaspoon salt

Dissolve yeast in lukewarm water. Warm the milk to temperature of the water, and add to dissolved yeast with sugar and shortening. Beat eggs well and add to liquid. Sift flour and salt together and stir into liquid mixture. Dough will be fairly stiff. Mix well and cover with a tea towel. Let rise in a warm place for 2 hours. Grease a large angel-food cake pan (10-inch tube pan). Punch dough down and place in greased pan. Cover and let rise to within an inch of the top. Place in a cold oven and turn oven to 350°. Bake for about 1 hour. Serve piping hot. Sally Lunn is delicious sliced when cold, buttered and toasted.

Miney's Coffee Cake

{Adapted from "A rich cake," American Cookery, 1796}

2 cakes of fresh yeast
1 tablespoon plus 1¾ cups sugar
2 cups lukewarm milk (80° to
   90°)
3½ cups flour

3 eggs
4 ounces raisins
4 tablespoons ground cinnamon
¼ cup melted butter

Dissolve yeast and 1 tablespoon sugar in the lukewarm milk. Add 1½ cups flour; beat well. Let stand for 1 hour, or until light. Beat eggs. Add 1½ cups of sugar, the eggs and remainder of flour. Stir and mix well. Pour into well-buttered 9-inch pie pans so that dough is no more than 1 inch thick. Press raisins into dough about 1 inch apart. Let cakes rise at room temperature until they double in height. Mix cinnamon and remaining ¼ cup sugar and sprinkle thickly over cakes. Then sprinkle with melted butter. Bake at 350° as you would layer cakes, until cakes spring back to the touch and a wooden pick inserted comes out clean, 25 to 40 minutes. *Makes 5 cakes.*

AMERICAN IRON TOASTER

✳ Apple Muffins or Pancakes

{ Adapted from "To Make Fine Fritters," The Art of Cookery, 1796 }

1¼ cups flour
1 tablespoon plus 2 teaspoons
   granulated sugar
2 tablespoons brown sugar
½ teaspoon salt
¼ teaspoon baking soda
3 tablespoons baking powder
1 apple, peeled, cored, and diced

⅛ teaspoon grated nutmeg
½ teaspoon ground cinnamon or
   mace
1 egg
½ cup sour milk or buttermilk
3 tablespoons melted shortening, or
   half bacon drippings, half
   shortening

19

Sift together the flour, 1 tablespoon granulated sugar and the brown sugar, salt, baking soda and baking powder. Dredge apple pieces with a mixture of remaining 2 teaspoons sugar, the nutmeg and cinnamon or mace together with a little of the flour mixture. Beat the egg and sour milk together, and add the dry ingredients. Fold in apple and melted shortening, and mix well. Pour into greased muffin tins and bake in a 400° oven for about 20 minutes.

To make pancakes, add enough more milk to make a thin batter. Drop spoonfuls onto a greased griddle, and fry until golden brown on both sides. *Makes 8 to 12.*

✷ Cranberry Nut Bread or Muffins

¾ cup sugar
1 egg
1¼ cups orange juice
1 tablespoon grated orange rind

3 cups dry biscuit mix
1 cup chopped cranberries
¾ cup chopped nuts

Mix sugar, egg, orange juice and rind together, and beat vigorously for about 1 minute. Add biscuit mix and blend well. Stir in cranberries and nuts. Pour into a well-greased loaf pan (9 x 5 inches), and bake in 350° oven for 55 to 60 minutes.

Make muffins by pouring into well-greased muffin pans, and bake until golden brown on top. *Makes 1 loaf or about 10 muffins.*

✷ Indian Cake or Bannock
{ *Adapted from "Indian Cake,"* The American Frugal Housewife, *1836* }

1 cup white cornmeal
½ cup flour
1 teaspoon salt
¼ teaspoon ground ginger
1 teaspoon baking soda

1 cup sour milk
1 egg
2 tablespoons molasses
3 tablespoons corn oil

Mix together cornmeal, flour, salt and ginger. Add baking soda to the sour milk, and pour liquid into the dry mixture. Beat egg and molasses together and then beat into first mixture, mixing well. Pour corn oil into batter and beat well. Turn into a well-greased loaf pan (8 x 4 inches), and bake in 425° oven for 25 minutes. Delicious when warm from the oven and equally good cold or spread with butter and reheated in the oven. Good with breakfast fruits and luncheon salads.

AMBER GLASS MILK BOWL

✱ Corn Bread with Variations

{Variation of "Indian Cake," The American Frugal Housewife, 1836}

½ cup flour
1 cup cornmeal, yellow or white
½ teaspoon baking soda
1 teaspoon salt

1 egg, beaten
1 cup buttermilk or sour milk
3 tablespoons bacon drippings

Mix dry ingredients well. Combine egg and buttermilk and beat thoroughly. Add to dry mixture, stirring only enough to blend. Add bacon drippings. Pour into a greased hot pan (7 x 11 inches), and bake in 450° oven for 20 to 25 minutes. Or pour into a greased hot 8-inch cast-iron skillet. Cook over low heat, covered, till almost dry on top, approximately 10 to 15 minutes. Turn to brown top for 3 or 4 minutes. Cut into pie-shaped pieces.

VARIATIONS
Mexican Corn Bread: Add to basic batter ½ cup grated rat cheese and ¼ to 1/3 cup jalapeño relish, *salsa piquante* or chopped green chilies. The amount will depend on your taste for hot, spicy bread. Increase the bacon grease to 1/3 cup and add another egg. Bake as usual. You can also include ½ cup cream-style corn in this mixture. If so, bake in 350° oven for 30 to 35 minutes.
Bacon Corn Bread: Fry 4 to 6 slices of bacon until crisp, drain, crumble, and add to basic batter. Bake as usual in pan or skillet greased with bacon drippings. You can also add ¼ cup chopped onion which has been sautéed.

✳ Grandmother Neuhaus' Parnash (Scrapple)

1 pound best bulk sausage available
(half hot and half mild if
desired)
3 cups water
½ teaspoon ground cloves

½ teaspoon white pepper
pinch of salt
pinch of ground allspice
2 cups yellow cornmeal
1 cup dry pancake mix

Put sausage and water in a *large* kettle and let come to a good boil. Add cloves, pepper, salt and allspice; then stir in cornmeal. Add pancake mix as fast as possible, stirring constantly. This will make a very stiff mixture. Grease heatproof glass loaf pans or baking dishes and pack *Parnash* into them tightly. Refrigerate for several hours. Cut into slices and fry in butter. Watch carefully as it burns easily. Serve with syrup for breakfast. Don't overlook supper possibilities; it's good accompanied by green or fruit salad. This can be frozen and keeps very well.

If a meatier Parnash is desired, increase the sausage proportions. *Makes 10 to 12 servings.*

ENGLISH PEWTER CANN—
"BRITTON'S FLOURISH"

✳ Fluffy Spoon Bread

{*Adapted from "Pan Corn Bread," Grosvenor, 1850*}

¾ cup cornmeal
2 cups milk, scalded
2 tablespoons butter

½ teaspoon salt
3 eggs, separated

Add cornmeal to scalded milk and cook slowly for about 5 minutes, until thickened. Add butter and salt, and let the mixture cool. Beat egg yolks well and mix. Whip eggs whites till stiff and fold into mixture. Pour into a buttered 1-quart soufflé dish, and bake in hot-water bath in 325° oven for 45 minutes. *Makes 6 servings.*

Scones

*{Adapted from "To Make Bisquits," New American
Cookery, 1805}*

2 cups flour	*4 tablespoons butter or margarine*
2 teaspoons baking powder	*2 eggs*
½ teaspoon salt	*½ cup light cream or milk*
2 teaspoons sugar	

Sift together the flour and baking powder with salt and sugar. Work in the butter with a pastry blender. Beat the eggs and cream together and mix into the other ingredients, making a soft but firm dough. It may be necessary to work in a little more cream. Knead on a floured board for about ½ minute, and roll out ¾-inch thick. Cut into pieces with a biscuit cutter and place on a greased cookie sheet. Bake in 450° oven for about 15 minutes, or until brown. If desired, add 1/3 cup softened dried currants before kneading.

Scones are traditionally served for tea with strawberry jam and clotted cream. Clotted cream is unavailable in many places, but a reasonable substitute can be made by blending 1 or 2 tablespoons of heavy cream with 3 ounces of cream cheese. *Makes 12 to 18.*

EARLY TEXAS
SPATTERWARE CHURN

Dinner

Early afternoon was the appointed hour for dinner in Colonial America. Throughout the seventeenth century and well into the eighteenth century it was served in the "hall" or "common room." This was, of course, the kitchen and had the added distinction of being the only room large enough to accommodate the whole family at mealtime. Often, long-winded graces were said as the family waited around the table upon which dinner was placed.

An early pioneer home was sadly lacking in comforts, and the family stood while eating. Their days were totally occupied with the necessary tasks of survival, and there was no time for making chairs, stools or other creature comforts. Despite the hardships, these stoic families never neglected to give thanks to God not only before meals but after as well.

Most of the adaptations in this book are based on receipts prepared for the wealthier Colonists who could afford exotic seasonings and the lavish use of dairy products. While dinner among the affluent merchants in the North took place shortly after noon, the Southern planters enjoyed their dinner as late as 3 or even 4 o'clock. Southerners usually made a great occasion over the meal as, more often than not, it included guests. While the family and their guests gathered for dinner, great pots of bubbling stew were carried into the fields to feed the slaves and laborers.

In the early settlements, poor families ate from trenchers filled from a common stewpot, with a bowl of coarse salt the only table adornment. The earliest trenchers in America, as in the Middle Ages, were probably made from slabs of stale bread which were either eaten with the meal or thrown after use to the domestic animals. The stews often included pork, sweet corn and cabbage, or other vegetables and roots which were available. A young Massachusetts boy's diary in 1797 speaks of winter rations as "beef-broth with brown bread and for a change bean porridge with pork (a handful of beans all boiled until 'smashed' and then bread crumbled in)." Sunday dinner for this young man consisted of baked beans and salt pork followed by baked Indian pudding with butter.

Throughout the Colonies dinner among the well-to-do was the beginning of social gatherings which continued more or less uninterrupted until bedtime. For example, in the cities, after a leisurely dinner followed by several rounds of Madeira, Port or cider, the gentlemen took themselves off to the coffeehouses for backgammon and cards. At five they broke up to call on the ladies at home for tea, and then it was off to the tavern for supper, bumpers of ale, and emotional orations on the vital topics of the day. In the Southern rural areas the plantations served as a meeting place for all these occasions. These romantic mansions had many rooms, enough for all "entertainments." Invited guests, usually consisting of whole families, arrived in the early afternoon in time for a bit of gossip for the ladies and cards for the men before dinner. On festive occasions, this meal would be served as late as 4:30 in the afternoon. The musicians would "strike up" directly after dinner for dancing. Cards would resume, drinking would continue, and laughter would resound from the taunting and teasing parlor games played by the young.

A typical comfortably fixed family in the late 1700s probably served two courses for dinner. The first course included several meats plus meat puddings and/or deep meat pies containing fruits and spices, pancakes and fritters, and the ever-present side dishes of sauces, pickles and catsups. Colonial catsups, of which there were many varieties, largely nut-flavored, were used as seasoning and were not tomato-based. Great batches were made at one time, for they could be stored for years. With all these tasty additives available, each diner was able to prepare his favorite sauce to complement the foods being served. The arrangements of dishes on the table and the garnishing of the platters were considered of the utmost importance. Garnishes included sippets (small toasts fried in butter), lemon slices on occasion, fried parsley and other herbs, bacon curls, capers, minced egg and horseradish.

The hog was the most common provider of meat to the early settled Colonials. When first introduced in America, this animal was forced to forage far afield for its food. This developed the extremely lean "razorback" hog which helps give today's famous Virginia ham its distinctive flavor. Cattle also had to fend for themselves, unfortunately, to the detriment of the texture and taste of their meat. Perhaps because of this, many beef "made dishes" (dishes requiring a number of ingredients specially prepared and often cooked in stages) were developed. "Bubble and Squeak," made of strips of meat and cabbage, was popular, and was one of the many ideas brought from England which were easily adaptable in the Colonies. There were beef hashes, ragouts, soups and minced pies. Leftovers, too, must have inspired interesting combinations just as they do today.

Etiquette, as pointed out by Sarah Harrison in *The Housekeeper's Pocket Book*, London, 1738, called for boiled meat to be served first, then baked, and last roasted. Some of these meats would have been "removes," a dish that was removed from the table and replaced by another variety during the same course. Roasts (more like our baked meats today) would usually appear in the second course along with fowl or fish. When called for, additional sauces were served. For example, there were those made of bread, mushroom or celery to accompany fowl. There were sauces of shrimps, oysters and lobster to complement larger fish dishes. Peas, or "pease" as they were then called, must have been plentiful and delicious and they seem to have been the most popular vegetable. Pease porridge, of nursery rhyme fame, was similar to today's split-pea soup. While vegetables were often served as garnishes and accompaniments to meat, fowl or fish dishes, there were several vegetable "made dishes." Two favorites were baked beans, probably an Indian invention, and "Hoppin' John," a South Carolina concoction of black-eyed peas or field peas, water, onions, salt pork, and salt and pepper.

Soups seem to have been served before or in conjunction with the first course. Desserts appeared with the second course. An assortment of fresh, cooked or dried fruits, custards, tarts and sweetmeats was usually available. "Sallats," though more popular at supper, sometimes were served at dinner and occasionally provided decoration in the center of the table.

Dinner in the 1800s became more definable and not unlike our main meal today, although the custom of serving a variety of many dishes con-

IRON WAFFLE IRON, 1820

Dinner

DUTCH BRASS
"BELL" CANDLESTICK

tinued for years among the wealthy. This custom resulted from a rule of etiquette which called for a sufficient assortment of food choices to please the personal tastes of all those gathered at the dinner table. Most dinner party hostesses today still make a point of serving something all the guests will like. Throughout the ages sharing the main meal of the day with others has been a popular social custom. It is interesting to note that in Anglo-Saxon times dining in private was considered a disgrace.

While social customs are fascinating, how the food tasted to these American pioneers is of equal interest. Highly spiced food was popular in all thirteen colonies. The early cooks used much larger quantities of strong flavorings such as mace and nutmeg than the twentieth-century cook would dream of using. The "high" taste of slightly spoiled meat was actually enjoyed by the early settlers. Garlic was not popular. Amelia Simmons in her cookbook warned, ". . . garlicks, tho' used by the French, are better adapted to the uses of medicine than cookery." The early American housewives were well aware of the medicinal values of herbs as well as their preservative and flavoring qualities. Early cookbooks include numerous recipes for herbal tonics, poultices and remedies.

As the earliest settlement phase drew to an end, butter and cheese were available to all but the very poor. Trade developed and spices became more affordable for the great majority of the people. These developments certainly improved the quality of table fare in Colonial life. Dr. Alexander Hamilton, a skeptical Scottish physician, wrote in 1744, as he traveled from Maryland up through New England, of a Boston Saturday dinner

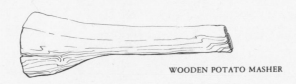

WOODEN POTATO MASHER

which consisted of salt codfish in a sauce of butter and eggs. On another occasion, anticipating a meal of clams, he exclaimed, "The landlady called for the bedpan. I could not guess what she intended to do with it, unless it was to warm her bed to go to sleep after dinner, but I found that it was used by way of a chafing dish to warm our dish of clams." Thanks to diligent diarists such as Dr. Hamilton, we are able to get a glimpse back in time and garner some understanding of how and what the American Colonists ate and "the way it was."

By the end of the 1700s sugar had become plentiful and its use dramatically changed desserts. In the eighteenth century a keg of brown sugar was worth a set of chairs, and four loaves of white sugar had the same value as a walnut chest. "Confectionaries" became the most popular desserts, replacing fruits, which continued to appear in pies and tarts and stuffings as well as with meat and fish dishes. Vanilla was soon widely used to scent and flavor sugar and was incorporated into desserts of all kinds.

Cakes were of many varieties: pound, gingerbread, spice and cheese. All stale cake was reserved for trifles and other concoctions. "Fool" and "flummery" were two popular custards. Jellies (flavored gelatins) in stemmed glasses arranged on pedestaled dishes were favorites with all ages. Jellies were also served with meats. Today we still use cranberry and mint jelly in this way. Mention is made of pine cones used as seasoning in pastries, and it was pointed out that they were beneficial for sore throats. Hazelnuts were thought to stimulate the appetite. Sweetmeats, pretty bite-sized delicacies, were almost always offered at the end of the meal. Many were made from chopped candied fruits, nuts or flowers. Peppermint drops, "comfit" (sugared roots and seeds), and "suckets" (candied lemon peels) were among the most popular of these treats. It is hard to distinguish between sweetmeats and "dainties," which were known as secondary desserts. "Dainties" were usually macaroons, quinces, sugared raisins, sweet relishes and sliced fresh fruits. All of these delicacies were served in

ENGLISH SHEFFIELD
SUGAR CASTER, 1800

HORN BEAKER

special dishes and great care was taken to arrange them in a pleasing fashion.

Wealthy Marylanders may have introduced ice cream to this country around 1744, for there is reference to it in writings in that colony. Pewter ice-cream machines soon appeared in the homes of the gentry. In large cities there were shops where ice cream could be purchased as a special treat. Shops selling baked goods also sprang up in the cities, which was a great help to the busy mistress of the house as well as to the coffeehouses, taverns and inns. Some women baked in their homes and sold their goods by advertising in the newspapers.

William Byrd II kept a remarkable "secret" diary from 1709 to 1712, written mostly at his home, Westover, in Virginia. While of great historical significance, shedding light on the daily life of one of the great plantation owners, it is of modest value to this treatise. William Byrd II, unfortunately, was the willing victim of a self-inflicted diet of meat and milk. Of interest here is the fact that diet crazes bewitched Colonial Americans as they do twentieth-century Americans. He does mention eating in the French manner, which probably referred to the custom of having the host slice the meat at a side table, put it on dinner plates and hand it to a servant, who then gave it to the mistress, who added vegetables. The servant, then placed each plate ceremoniously in front of the diner. Byrd also mentions one particularly good meat which had been "rendered tender" by long hours of soaking in vinegar. He also mentions a friend's cook who had a "fine secret means" of preserving meats.

Preparing a Colonial dinner was most assuredly a full-time job. Whether it was with the help of indentured servants, slaves, or only family aid, it was a serious, time-consuming business and never the slapdash method family cooks fall prey to in modern America. Perhaps there is a need today for the creative homemaker to spend more time in the kitchen, improving nutrition, flavor and eye appeal.

Indeed, the proof of a better pudding will result in better eating!

29

✻❀✻ To broil Crimp-Cod, Salmon, Whiting, or Haddock

Flour it, have a quick clear fire and set your gridiron high, broil it of a fine brown, lay it in your dish, and for sauce have good melted butter; take a lobster, bruise the spawn in the butter, cut the meat small, put all together into the melted butter, make it hot and pour it into your dish or into basons. Garnish with horse-radish and lemon.

The Art of Cookery Made Plain and Easy
Hannah Glasse, 1796

✻ Basic Procedures with Fish

{ *Adapted from "Stewed Fish,"* Grosvenor, 1850, *and "To Broil Crimp-Cod, Salmon, Whiting or Haddock,"* The Art of Cookery, *1796*}

Fillets of fresh sole, trout, or any delicate white fish. Sprinkle with lemon juice and salt and let stand for 20 to 30 minutes.

TO PANBROIL
Melt butter in skillet. When hot, place fish in butter and cook till lightly browned. Turn once to brown other side; do not overcook; when fish flakes easily, it is done. Remove to a hot platter. Pour a little dry white wine into skillet to deglaze. Reduce to the amount sufficient for about 1 teaspoon to pour over each fillet. Serve with thin slices of lemon, or top with shaved almonds or sliced mushrooms that have been lightly browned in butter.

TO POACH
Place fish in a shallow oven dish. Cover with fish stock or a mixture of half dry white wine and half water with a slice of onion; cover. Cook in 350° oven for 12 to 15 minutes, or just until fish tests done. Remove to hot dish and dress as follows:

Florentine: Spread Béchamel sauce on bottom of a buttered ovenproof serving dish. Arrange poached fish on sauce. Spread fish with cooked chopped spinach. Pour over more sauce, sprinkle with freshly grated Parmesan cheese, and brown under broiler. Serve at once.

Véronique: Season cream sauce with a little white pepper, 1 teaspoon white wine, a drop or two of lemon juice and a dash of garlic salt. Add a little additional butter. In an ovenproof serving dish arrange poached fish fillets, pour over the sauce, and arrange skinned and seeded white grapes at each end. Run under the broiler for a few minutes to heat.

Marguery: Have ready cooked shrimps and lump crab meat, warmed in melted butter and seasoned with onion salt. Arrange poached fish fillets in an ovenproof serving dish; put the shrimps and crab over the fish, reserving butter. Pour cream sauce over the top, melted butter over all, and run under the broiler to brown.

SILVER SOUP SPOON

SILVER DESSERT SPOON MADE BY SLAVE "GARNET" IN KENTUCKY FOR ELIZA CARTER

✳ Pescado Olé

{*Variation of "To Broil Crimp-Cod . . .,"* The Art of Cookery, *1796*}

2 pounds red snapper steaks
salt and pepper
juice of 1 lemon
1 garlic clove, minced
2 medium-size onions, sliced
4 tablespoons olive oil

1 can (1 pound) peeled tomatoes
4 tablespoons chopped ripe olives
2 to 3 tablespoons capers
2 to 4 jalapeño peppers, seeded and
* chopped fine*

Season fish with salt and pepper, and sprinkle with lemon juice. Set aside. In a large skillet sauté the garlic and onions in olive oil until limp. Add tomatoes, olives, capers and jalapeño peppers (the amount according to your taste), and simmer slowly till thick. Add fish fillets, cover with sauce, and cook till fish is just flaky. Remove fish to a hot platter and cook sauce quickly to thicken it again, stirring constantly. Spoon sauce over fish and serve with saffron rice. *Makes 6 servings.*

✳ Deviled Crab with Avocados

{ *Variation on "Crabs Dressed,"* The Practical
Housewife, *1860*}

2 ripe avocados
½ cup white-wine vinegar
2 small garlic cloves, cut into pieces
6 tablespoons butter or margarine
5 tablespoons flour
3 cups milk
3 cups Alaskan King crab meat
1 teaspoon creole-type prepared
   mustard

2 teaspoons salt
3 tablespoons lemon juice
2 teaspoons Worcestershire sauce
2 tablespoons minced parsley
⅓ cup sherry or brandy
1 cup shredded sharp Cheddar cheese

Peel avocados and cut into large slices. Place in a flat dish and sprinkle well with white-wine vinegar. Scatter pieces of garlic around in the vinegar (they will be removed later); let avocados stand in vinegar for about 30 minutes, turning slices occasionally. Meanwhile, melt the butter, add flour, and stir over medium heat to blend well. Add milk gradually, stirring constantly until mixture is thickened. Stir in crab meat, mustard, salt, lemon juice, Worcestershire sauce, parsley, and sherry or brandy.

Pour off the vinegar from the avocados and discard the pieces of garlic. Arrange the avocado pieces in a baking dish. Spoon the hot crab mixture over the avocado, using all of the sauce. Sprinkle shredded cheese over the sauce. Place in a 325° oven until the avocados are just heated through and the cheese is melted, about 10 minutes; do not overbake, or the avocados will lose their good flavor and may get a bit tough. *Makes 6 servings.*

ENGLISH IRON BREAD PEEL

✳ Scalloped Oysters

{ *Adapted from "Escaloped Oysters,"* The American
Frugal Housewife, *1836*}

1 quart shelled fresh oysters
2 ⅓ cups cracker crumbs
salt and pepper
grated mace

¼ pound butter
⅓ cup light cream
⅓ cup oyster liquid

Drain oysters and reserve oyster liquid. Set aside 2 rounded tablespoons of cracker crumbs for topping. In a buttered 6-cup casserole, spread a thin layer of cracker crumbs, then a layer of oysters. Sprinkle salt and pepper to taste and a dash of mace over oysters. Cover with a layer of cracker crumbs and dot with some of the butter. Continue layering until oysters and crumbs are all used. When all oysters and seasonings are used, and before final cracker crumbs are added, pour over the casserole the cream and oyster liquid which have been mixed together. Then add the top layer of crumbs and dot with butter. Bake in 350° oven for 35 minutes. *Makes 4 servings.*

VARIATION

For a different and even better flavor, use the same method, but omit the mace. Instead shake a few drops of Worcestershire sauce over each layer of oysters.

WOODEN SAUSAGE STUFFER

✳ Grady Smith's Oyster Jambalaya

{ *Traditional Louisiana* }

3½ cups raw rice
3 pints small oysters with liquor
8 slices of bacon
¼ pound butter
2 cups finely chopped onions
3½ cups chopped celery leaves

4 garlic cloves, chopped fine
24 whole allspice berries tied in
    cheesecloth bag
pepper and salt
Tabasco and Worcestershire sauce
1 cup chopped parsley

Cook the rice until fluffy and dry; set aside. Drain oysters and save liquor. Fry the bacon until crisp, drain, and crumble. Put the butter and half of the bacon grease in a large skillet and lightly brown the onions, celery leaves and garlic, over medium heat. Add allspice berries, seasonings to taste, then oysters, and cook slowly until oysters crinkle. Put cooked rice in a large pot set over or into hot water. Remove bag of allspice berries. Pour oysters, oyster liquor and parsley into rice, and mix gently and carefully. If there is too much liquid, add only a little at a time until you have the consistency of a nice gravy. It should not be runny! Add crumbled bacon on top just before serving. Serve with a green salad, crisp French bread and butter, and a good cheese and wine. *Makes 8 servings.*

❋ Apple Shrimp Curry

{ *Adapted from "To Make a Dish of Curry after the East Indian Manner,"* The Virginia Housewife, *1824*}

⅓ cup plus ½ cup butter
3 tablespoons chopped onion
3 tablespoons chopped celery
3 tablespoons chopped green apple
6 peppercorns
1 bay leaf
⅓ cup flour

2½ teaspoons curry powder
¼ teaspoon sugar
⅓ teaspoon grated nutmeg
2½ cups milk
2 teaspoons lemon juice
½ teaspoon Worcestershire sauce
1½ pounds cooked cleaned shrimps

Melt 1/3 cup butter in a heavy 3-quart saucepan. Add onion, celery, apple, peppercorns and bay leaf; cook over medium heat until onion is golden. Blend in mixture of flour, curry powder, sugar and nutmeg. Heat till mixture bubbles, stirring well. Remove from heat and add milk, mixing well. Return to heat and stir until thick. Add lemon juice and Worcestershire, and remove from heat. Let cool, remove bay leaf, and blend sauce, including peppercorns, in blender. Meantime, heat remaining ½ cup butter in a skillet and add cooked shrimps. Turn in butter to coat well, but do not cook. Pour into sauce and heat well. Serve over fluffy white rice or saffron rice. Accompany with the following condiments: grated coconut, chutney, chopped or blanched and slivered almonds, chopped fine cucumber, golden raisins, plumped in steam, hard-cooked eggs, whites and yolks chopped separately. *Makes 6 servings.*

❋ Shrimp Mold

{ *Variation of "Crawfish in Savoury Jelly,"* The Experienced English Housekeeper, *1794*}

1 envelope unflavored gelatin
¼ cup cold water
1 cup hot water
¼ cup lemon juice
½ teaspoon salt

⅛ teaspoon cayenne pepper
1 tablespoon sugar
2 tablespoons chili sauce
1 cup cooked cleaned shrimps
½ cup sweet pickle relish

Soften gelatin in the cold water. Add the hot water and stir till gelatin is completely dissolved. Add all other ingredients except shrimps and pickle relish. Let cool in refrigerator till thick but not set. Stir in shrimps and pickle relish, and adjust seasonings if necessary. Pour into a 3-cup mold and refrigerate till set. Serve garnished with artichoke hearts and the dressing below. *Makes 4 or 5 servings.*

DRESSING

⅓ *cup mayonnaise*   *1 tablespoon prepared horseradish*
⅓ *cup sour cream*

Mix together, and chill until serving time.

✳ Salmon Loaf

{ *Variation of "Crawfish in Savoury Jelly," The* Experienced English Housekeeper, *1794*}

4 egg yolks (see Note)   *2 envelopes unflavored gelatin*
2 tablespoons sugar   *1 cup cold water*
2 tablespoons dry mustard   *4 tablespoons vinegar*
1 teaspoon salt   *2 cans (7 ounces each) salmon*
2 cups milk

Beat egg yolks with sugar, mustard and salt. Add milk and cook over hot water, stirring constantly, until custard is thick. Soften gelatin in the cold water, add vinegar, and mix with hot custard. Bone, skin, and flake the salmon. Gently fold salmon into custard. Pour into an oiled 6-cup mold and refrigerate overnight.

Unmold on a serving dish. Garnish with sprigs of fresh dill or parsley and thin lemon slices. Serve with cucumber sauce (recipe follows). *Makes 6 servings.*

CUCUMBER SAUCE

3 to 4 tablespoons mayonnaise   *1 cup sour cream*
1 small cucumber, unpeeled, grated   *salt*
  and squeezed dry

Mix first three ingredients, and season with salt to taste.

NOTE
Save the egg whites to use in other dishes; for example, make meringues to fill with fresh fruit and cream for dessert. Also, egg whites freeze well.

✳ Brewer's Pot Roast à la Mode

{*Variation of "To Make Beef à la Mode,"* The Art of Cookery, *1796*}

5 *pounds beef pot roast (chuck, shoulder, etc.)*	2 *cans (12 ounces each) beer*
salt	2 *garlic cloves, sliced*
1 *piece of fresh gingerroot, sliced,*	1 *bay leaf*
or	1 *tablespoon peppercorns*
2 *teaspoons ground ginger*	2 *tablespoons cornstarch*
	¼ *cup hot water*

Rub roast well with salt; if using ground ginger, rub it in at this time. Place meat in a deep enamelware or glass pot and add other ingredients except cornstarch and hot water. Cover and refrigerate overnight, turning meat once. Remove meat from marinade and place in a shallow pan under a hot broiler. Sear and brown well on each side. Return to marinade, cover, and bake in 325° oven for 3½ to 4 hours, till fork tender. Remove to a hot dish, strain broth, and skim off any fat. Thicken with the cornstarch dissolved in the hot water. Correct seasonings and serve gravy over meat. If desired, vegetables such as potato, carrot and onion may be added during last hour of cooking. Turn and baste vegetables at least once during cooking so they are covered with the gravy. *Makes 8 to 10 servings.*

✳ Boeuf à la Vinaigrette

{*Variation of "Beef à la Mode,"* The Art of Cookery, *1796*}

3½ to 4 *pounds boneless beef roast*	1 *bunch of green onions with tops, chopped fine*
fat for browning	
salt	1 *green pepper, chopped fine*
1 *garlic clove*	¼ *cup chopped parsley*
1 *cup olive oil*	⅓ *teaspoon ground cuminseed*
⅓ *cup tarragon vinegar*	

Brown meat slightly in a little fat in a heavy pan. Sprinkle with salt and add garlic. Cover tightly with foil. Bake in 325° oven for about 2 hours, till fork-tender. Cool thoroughly and slice on the diagonal into very thin slices. Mix rest of the ingredients and layer with the beef slices in a flat dish. Let stand, covered, in the refrigerator for 24 hours. Serve cold with a hot potato salad or scalloped potatoes, cold tomato slices, cheese and crusty French bread. *Makes 6 to 8 servings.*

✳ Beef Braised with Green Peppercorns

{Variation of Beef à la Mode," The Art of Cookery, *1796}*

4 to 5 pounds boneless beef roast
   (bottom round or chuck)
salt
2 to 4 tablespoons olive oil
2 cups red wine
1 cup beef bouillon or strong stock

½ cup sliced onion
1 garlic clove, mashed
¼ teaspoon grated nutmeg
2 tablespoons green peppercorns
3 tablespoons chopped parsley

Rub meat with salt, and brown in oil on all sides. Pour off any excess oil and add other ingredients except peppercorns and half of parsley. Cook in 350° oven for 2 to 3 hours, basting frequently and turning several times. When meat is tender, remove from pan and let rest for 10 minutes. Meanwhile, reduce liquid over high heat to about ¾ cup; add peppercorns and rest of parsley. Slice meat very thin and arrange on a hot platter. Pour sauce over it.

This amount of sauce is very little for a roast of this size. If more sauce is desired, it can be made easily by boiling ½ cup beef stock or bouillon, 1 cup red wine and 1 tablespoon green peppercorns till reduced by half. Thicken with ½ teaspoon cornstarch that has been dissolved in 1 tablespoon cold water. Add to pan juices. *Makes 8 to 10 servings.*

PEWTER AND
WOOD LADLE, 1750

✻❀✻ *Veal Olives*

Take the bone out of the fillet and cut thin slices the size of the leg, beat them flat, rub them with the yelk of an egg beaten, lay on each piece a thin slice of boiled ham, sprinkle salt, pepper, grated nutmeg, chopped parsley, and bread crumbs over all, roll them up tight, and secure them with skewers, rub them with egg and roll them in bread crumbs, lay them on a tin dripping pan, and set them in an oven; when brown on one side, turn them, and when sufficiently done, lay them in a rich highly seasoned gravy made of proper thickness, stew them till tender, garnish with forcemeat balls and green pickles sliced.

The Virginia Housewife: or, Methodical Cook
Mrs. Mary Randolph, 1824

✻ Veal or Beef "Olives"

{ *Adapted from "Veal Olives,"* The Virginia Housewife, *1824* }

veal cutlets, beef cutlets, or beef flank cut into pieces about 5 inches long and 3-4 inch wide
Dijon mustard
sour pickles

beef stock or hot water
bacon or thin ham slices
flour, butter or bacon fat
sour cream
salt

No exact proportions are given in this recipe because each "olive" is prepared separately according to taste. Allow two per person.

For each "olive," spread meat with mustard; slice pickles lengthwise and place 1 slice on meat. Cover with 2 slices of bacon or 1 ham slice and roll the meat over the pickle and ham. Secure with wooden picks. Heat butter in a heavy skillet and brown olives well. Cover tightly and let simmer over *low* heat for about 1 hour. If absolutely necessary, add stock or hot water, 1 tablespoon at a time, if meat starts to burn or stick. When tender, remove meat to a hot platter. Add flour to pan juices to make a roux, and some beef stock to make thick gravy. Lastly stir in sour cream and taste for salt. Serve with sauce poured over meat, and accompany with buttered hot noodles.

Dinner

✳ Barbecued Beef Brisket

{*Variation of "Beef à la Mode,"* The Art of Cookery, 1796}

5 pounds beef brisket
2 tablespoons liquid hickory-
   smoked seasoning
1 teaspoon onion salt

1 teaspoon celery salt
1 teaspoon garlic salt
2 tablespoons Worcestershire sauce
cracked pepper

Place brisket in heavy foil on a large flat pan. Season with smoked season-ing, onion salt, celery salt and garlic salt, and seal tightly. Refrigerate overnight. Next day, add Worcestershire sauce and cracked pepper to taste, and reseal. Bake at 250° for 5 to 6 hours. Serve hot or cold. Slice on the diagonal and serve with horseradish and sour-cream sauce (recipe follows). *Makes 8 servings.*

VARIATION
Try about 6 tablespoons of soy sauce sprinkled on both sides and 1 table-spoon ground ginger. No other seasoning is necessary unless you wish to add pepper. This version is good hot.

HORSERADISH AND SOUR-CREAM SAUCE
To 1 cup sour cream, add 4 to 6 tablespoons grated horseradish, according to taste.

✳ Mod London Broil

½ tablespoon monosodium
   glutamate
½ tablespoon salt
1 teaspoon sugar
1 tablespoon instant minced onion
½ teaspoon dry mustard
½ teaspoon ground rosemary

¼ teaspoon ground ginger
1 teaspoon whole peppercorns
¼ cup lemon juice
½ cup salad oil
1 garlic clove, split
1½ to 2 pounds beef flank steak

Mix all ingredients except beef to form a marinade. Place beef in a shallow glass dish and pour marinade over it. Allow to stand in refriger-ator for 3 to 4 hours, turning meat several times. Remove meat from marinade and place on broiler rack 4 to 5 inches from source of heat. Broil for 5 minutes on each side. Carve steak into very thin slices diagon-ally across the grain. *Makes 3 or 4 servings. When used as an appetizer, this will make 3 to 4 dozen small pieces.*

VARIATION

⅓ cup soy sauce
⅓ cup dry sherry
2 green onions with tops, chopped

⅓ cup oil
peppercorns

For an alternate marinade, mix first four ingredients, and add peppercorns to taste.

AMERICAN PEWTER
CREAM POT

✳ Baked Steak Stuffed with Rice

{ *Variation of "Ragout,"* Grosvenor, 1850 }

2 pounds beef round steak
flour seasoned with salt and pepper
⅓ cup fine-chopped onion
2 tablespoons fat
2 tablespoons flour
¼ cup seasoned tomato juice
¼ teaspoon ground thyme
½ teaspoon ground marjoram
¼ teaspoon ground summer savory

2 cups cooked brown rice
chopped parsley
butter or fat for browning
3 slices of bacon
2 cups beef stock or hot water
½ cup dry red wine
cornstarch (optional)
1 tablespoon currant jelly

Pound steak thoroughly with seasoned flour. Set aside. Brown onion slightly in fat, add the 2 tablespoons flour, and stir to make a roux. Add seasoned tomato juice and herbs, and cook for 10 minutes or so. Add cooked rice and as much parsley as you like; stir to mix thoroughly. Spread this mixture over the steak, roll it, and fasten with skewers or tie well with cord. Brown steak thoroughly on all sides in a small amount of butter or fat. Place the roulade in a baking dish and arrange bacon slices over the top. Add beef stock or water. Cook in 325° oven for 2 hours. Remove to a heated platter. To the baking juices add the wine, thicken slightly with cornstarch if needed, and add the currant jelly. Stir well. Allow steak to cool for about 10 minutes before carving. Serve with the sauce made from pan juices. *Makes 4 to 6 servings.*

✳ Veal or Chicken Hash

{ *Adapted from "To Hash Veal,"* The Art of Cookery, *1796* }

2 tablespoons chopped onion
2 tablespoons butter or margarine
2 cups diced leftover veal or
  chicken
1 cup leftover gravy or thickened
  chicken stock

grated rind of 1 lemon
3 tablespoons capers
1 tablespoon chopped parsley
¼ cup heavy cream
½ teaspoon cornstarch (if
  necessary)

Sauté onion in butter until golden. Add rest of ingredients except cream and cornstarch, and simmer until meat is hot. Just before serving, stir in cream but don't boil. If hash is too liquid, thicken with cornstarch before adding cream. Serve in pastry shells or on toasted rounds of buttered French bread. Also good with spoon bread. *Makes 3 or 4 servings.*

VARIATION
To make a more elegant dish, sauté 1 cup of sliced mushrooms with the onions and proceed as above.

✳ Tweedy Family Steak
and Kidney Pie

2 pounds beef or veal, round or
  sirloin steak
1 beef kidney, or 2 small veal
  kidneys
2 tablespoons flour
½ teaspoon minced sweet basil

¼ teaspoon minced summer savory
salt and pepper
1 large onion, chopped
2 tablespoons butter
double recipe Basic Pastry (p. 72)

Cut beef into ½-inch cubes. Wash and trim kidney and cut into small pieces. Mix meats with flour, herbs, seasonings to taste and chopped onion. Brown in butter in a deep skillet. Add water to cover and cook slowly until meat is tender and gravy thick.

Line a deep heatproof glass or other ovenware dish, about 2-quart size, with pastry. Fill with meat mixture. Cover top with another sheet of pastry, seal edges, cut steam vents, and bake in 400° oven till brown. Serve with hot English mustard and plenty of beer. *Makes 8 servings.*

✳ Aromatic Stew

2 tablespoons cooking oil
2 tablespoons butter
3½ to 4 pounds beef, cut into 1-
inch cubes
1 medium-sized onion, sliced thin
½ tablespoon salt

1 tablespoon Angostura bitters
⅓ cup chopped parsley
½ cup stuffed small olives
½ cup golden raisins
1 cup dry sherry

In a heavy skillet heat the oil and butter; add beef cubes and brown well. Add onion rings and continue browning until onion is limp. Add rest of ingredients and cover tightly. Cook in 325° oven for about 1½ hours, adding a little water if meat cooks dry. Serve over hot cooked rice. *Makes 6 to 8 servings.*

PEWTER MASTER SALT
AND GUARD SPOONS

Ropa Vieja

{ *Adapted from "Ropa Vieja—Spanish,"* The Virginia Housewife, *1824* }

2 pounds beef flank steak
2 garlic cloves, crushed
1 large green pepper, cut into strips
1 medium-sized onion, cut into
lengthwise strips
3 cherry tomatoes, or 1 small
tomato

salt and pepper
⅓ cup oil
1 cup canned tomato sauce
½ cup red wine
1 bay leaf
1 can (4 ounces) pimientos, cut into
small strips

Boil flank steak in enough water to cover, seasoning it with 1 garlic clove, a few strips of green pepper and onion, tomatoes, and salt and pepper to taste. Boil for 2 to 3 hours, or until the meat is tender; drain. Shred the meat with the grain; set aside. Sauté the other garlic clove, remaining onion and green pepper in the oil until limp. Add tomato sauce, wine, bay leaf, pimientos and 1 teaspoon salt, and cook for 5 minutes. Add meat and cook for an additional 25 to 30 minutes. Remove bay leaf. Serve over rice. *Makes 4 servings.*

✳ Forcemeat Balls à la Grecque

{ *Variation of "Forcemeat Balls," The Virginia Housewife, 1824* }

2 pounds beef or veal, ground
2 small onions, chopped fine
½ cup raw rice
salt and pepper
½ cup flour

2 cups water
2 tablespoons oil or butter
Lemon Sauce (recipe follows)
4 tablespoons chopped mixed mint
    and parsley

Mix well meat, onions, rice, and salt and pepper to taste. Shape into small balls and roll gently in flour. In a saucepan bring water to a boil with oil or butter and a little salt. Add meatballs and simmer for 35 to 40 minutes. Remove to a hot platter. Serve with lemon sauce, sprinkled with mint and parsley. Delicious with noodles or rice and a good tossed salad that includes Kalamata olives, radishes and Feta cheese. *Makes 4 to 6 servings.*

LEMON SAUCE

3 eggs, separated
juice of 2 lemons
1 cup broth (use liquid in which
    meatballs were cooked)

1 tablespoon cornstarch

Beat egg whites until stiff. Add egg yolks and continue beating. Add lemon juice *slowly*, and beat constantly so that sauce does not curdle. Thicken broth with cornstarch and add slowly to egg mixture. Continue beating over low heat until smooth and thick.

✳ Chile con Carne

6 to 8 tablespoons bacon drippings
3 pounds beef chuck, or 1 pound
    beef chuck and 2 pounds
    venison, chile-ground (see Note)
2 large onions, chopped
3 to 4 cups hot water or beef stock
3 or 4 large garlic cloves, mashed
3 to 4 tablespoons chili powder

2 tablespoons paprika
1 tablespoon salt
1 tablespoon ground cuminseed
½ tablespoon ground coriander
1 teaspoon black pepper
¼ teaspoon sugar
1 can (16 ounces) red kidney beans
    (see Note)

Heat a Dutch oven. Melt bacon drippings. If beef is very lean, use 2 to 4 tablespoons additional bacon fat. Brown meat well, stirring and chopping to separate. Add onions during last 5 minutes of browning. Add water and all other ingredients except beans. Add chili powder a little at a time to adjust to the amount of hotness desired. Cover and simmer for 4 to 5 hours, stirring occasionally and adding additional beef stock or water if necessary. When done, add beans with their liquid and cook for about 30 minutes longer.

Serve *chile* with guacamole salad, toasted tortillas, cold beer, and flan for dessert. Keep a pretty bouquet of parsley, with grape shears, nearby after coffee, so that the guests can nibble and "de-garlic" after dinner! *Makes 8 servings.*

Note Meat that is "chile-ground" has been put through the coarsest blade of the food grinder; the meat remains in little chunks rather than tiny bits. Beef used for *chile* should contain more fat than regular ground chuck.

If you prefer *chile* without beans, thicken the *chile* after cooking with 1/3 cup flour mixed well into 1/3 cup water. Add this mixture to *chile* over low heat and stir *constantly* for several minutes until it thickens liquid.

✳ Royal Mincemeat

{ *Adapted from "Another Method of Making Mince Pies,"* The Housekeeper's Instructor, *1798* }

2 pounds lean beef or venison	2½ cups sugar
2 pounds tongue	2 teaspoons salt
1 pound suet	2 teaspoons grated nutmeg
4 cups seedless raisins	2 teaspoons ground allspice
2 cups dried currants	1 teaspoon ground cloves
1 cup chopped citron	3 bottles brandy, approximately
1 cup chopped orange peel	1 bottle sherry
½ cup chopped figs	

Cover beef (or venison) and tongue with water in a saucepan. Simmer until tender, about 3 hours. Pour off water and grind meats with suet, using coarse grinder blade. Add remaining ingredients except alcohol and mix well. Add enough brandy, about 3 fifths, to make a thick soupy mixture. Place in a crock, cover loosely, and let stand at room temperature for about 2 weeks. Check to see if liquid is absorbed and add sherry to moisten. Check regularly, adding sherry if needed. Should stand for 6 months before it is really good.

When using in pie, add chopped peeled apples in an amount roughly equal to mincemeat. (Old tradition is to serve this as a main course. Add cheese, salad and good light red wine.) *Makes about 5 quarts.*

✲❀✲ *To make little Pasties to fry*

Take the kidney of a loin of veal or lamb, fat and all, shred it very small, season it with a little salt, cloves, mace, nutmeg, all beaten small, some sugar, and the yolks of two or three hard eggs, minc'd very fine; mix all these together with a little sack or cream; put them in puff-paste and fry them; serve them hot.

The Compleat Housewife: or Accomplish'd Gentle-woman's Companion
E. Smith, 1744

✲ Meat Pasties

{ *Adapted from "To Make Little Pasties to Fry,"* The Compleat Housewife, *1744* }

FILLING
1½ tablespoons chopped green
  onions, tops included
2 tablespoons butter
1 cup diced cooked ham, chicken,
  turkey or duck
3 tablespoons dry sherry

⅓ cup dry white wine
½ teaspoon dried herb: rosemary
  with ham; tarragon with chicken
  or turkey; orégano with duck
salt and pepper

Sauté onions in butter until limp. Add meat and cook slightly. Add sherry and white wine and cook till liquid has almost evaporated. Add herbs, and season with salt and pepper to taste. Set aside.

45

SAUCE

2 tablespoons butter	salt and pepper
2½ tablespoons flour	1 egg yolk
1 cup boiling liquid, ½ cup milk or	¼ cup heavy cream
light cream and ½ cup stock	

Make a roux with butter and flour, stir till smooth. Very slowly add boiling liquid and stir till thick and smooth. Season. Beat together the egg yolk and cream and slowly beat into the cream sauce, then add meat mixture. Should be quite thick.

Use your favorite pastry recipe (see Sour-Cream Pastry); roll dough into a rectangle about 1/8 inch thick. Cut into 6-inch squares and put 2 good tablespoons of filling on each square. Fold to make a triangle and moisten inside edges, pressing together with tines of fork to seal. Place on a buttered baking sheet. Beat together 1 egg yolk and 1 teaspoon water. Brush each pasty with this mixture and cut an X in top for steam vent. Bake in 425° oven for 28 minutes.

For canapés, cut pastry into 2½-inch squares. Place 1 teaspoon filling in each, form a triangle, brush with egg mix, and cut an X. Bake at 425° for 15 minutes.

Can be frozen; reheat, unthawed, in 425° oven until hot.

✳ Fruited Pork Chops

{ *Variation on "Broiling Pork Chops,"* The Housekeeper's Instructor, *1798* }

6 double pork chops, butterflied	½ cup pineapple juice
salt	½ cup honey
butter	2 tablespoons dry mustard
12 coriander seeds	⅛ teaspoon ground cloves
2 cups brown sugar	

Sprinkle chops with salt and brown in small amount of butter. Crush coriander seeds and mix with rest of ingredients to make a sauce; pour over chops. Bake in 350° oven, basting frequently, for about 1 hour. Keep covered with aluminum foil between bastings. Garnish with a wooden pick on which you spear an orange slice, a lemon slice, a cube of pineapple and a cherry. Serve with Brown Rice Pilau (see Index). *Makes 6 servings.*

✳ Liver in Wine Sauce

{ *Inspired by "A Ragoo of Livers," The Art of Cookery, 1796* }

5 to 6 tablespoons butter
1 tablespoon olive oil
1 large onion, chopped
1 garlic clove, crushed
½ pound liver, sliced ½ inch thick
　and cut into 1-inch strips
flour seasoned with salt and pepper

1 tablespoon orange juice
grated rind of 1 orange
¼ cup Dubonnet or cream sherry or
　Madeira
2 tablespoons chopped parsley
thin lemon slices

Melt butter and oil in a heavy skillet. Sauté onion and garlic until soft and golden. Dredge liver pieces with seasoned flour and sauté in the same skillet until golden and just done. Remove from pan to a heated dish. Mix orange juice and grated rind, wine and half of parsley together. Pour into skillet to deglaze and reduce liquid to about half. Pour over liver and sprinkle with rest of parsley. Garnish with very thin lemon slices. *Makes 4 servings.*

AMERICAN SILVER TABLESPOON,
JOHN W. CAMPBELL, NEW YORK, 1814

✳ Ham Roulades

2 cups boiling water
1 package (3 ounces) lemon-
　flavored gelatin
2 bouillon cubes
6 ounces cream cheese
1½ ounces Roquefort cheese

6 tablespoons horseradish, or less
1 teaspoon salt
dash of cayenne
⅓ cup whipped cream
14 thin slices of ham, rectangular
　in shape

Pour boiling water over lemon-flavored gelatin, add bouillon cubes, and stir until dissolved. Mix together cream cheese, Roquefort cheese, horse-radish, salt, cayenne and whipped cream. Mix well. Cut ham into ap-proximately 4-inch squares. Spread some of the mixture on each slice, and roll. Place rolls in a shallow pan, and cover with gelatin which has been allowed to thicken slightly. Let set in refrigerator. Serve with stuffed tomatoes and hot bread for a delicious lunch. Also good as a first course, served with thin-sliced brown bread and butter. *Makes 5 or 6 servings.*

✶ Adela's Corned-Beef Mousse

1 package (6 ounces) orange-or
  lemon-flavored gelatin
1 cup hot water
1 pound canned corned-beef hash,
  mashed
1 can (10½ ounces) condensed beef
  consommé, undiluted
1 cup mayonnaise
1 cup fine-chopped celery

1½ medium-size green peppers,
  chopped fine
3 green onions with tops, chopped
  fine
4 hard-cooked eggs, chopped
⅛ teaspoon salt
lettuce
4 tablespoons sour cream
12 slices of anchovy or stuffed olive

Make gelatin according to directions on the package, using the 1 cup hot water. Let cool and begin to set. Mix other ingredients except lettuce, sour cream and anchovies, and stir into gelatin. Pour into an oiled 2-quart soufflé dish, ring mold or casserole, or 12 individual molds. Let set in refrigerator. Unmold to serve on lettuce. Garnish each serving with 1 teaspoon sour cream topped by a slice of anchovy or stuffed olive. *Makes 12 servings.*

✶ Sour Rabbit and Potato Dumplings

1 rabbit, about 5 pounds
3 onions, sliced
2 to 3 cups white vinegar
22 to 26 allspice berries
12 peppercorns

4 cloves
6 bay leaves
1 teaspoon salt
butter or bacon fat
flour or cornstarch

Clean rabbit and cut into serving pieces. Layer rabbit pieces and onion slices alternately in a glass pan. Cover with vinegar. Tie spices and bay leaves in a cheesecloth bag and add along with the salt. Let the rabbit marinate, covered, in refrigerator overnight.

Remove rabbit pieces and brown well in a little butter or bacon fat in a heavy skillet. When browned, add a small portion of the marinade and onions; cover and cook slowly. Continue to add portions of marinade, diluted with half water, and some of the onions as meat cooks. Do not add too much liquid at any one time. When rabbit is tender, remove from pan. Add flour or cornstarch to pan liquid to thicken to a gravy. Adjust seasoning. Return rabbit to gravy. Serve with Potato Dumplings (recipe follows). *Makes 4 to 6 servings.*

✳ Potato Dumplings

6 *large white potatoes*
2 *eggs, well beaten*

3 *tablespoons flour*
1 *teaspoon baking powder*

Peel potatoes, cook and mash, using no seasonings, butter or milk. Add eggs, flour and baking powder to potatoes, and work together thoroughly on a floured board. Have ready a kettle of salt water, boiling. To test dough, break off a small piece and roll into a ball. Drop into boiling water and cook for about 12 minutes. If the dumpling comes to the top of the water and stays together, it has the right consistency. If it doesn't rise to the top, work a little more flour into the batter. If the dumpling rises but falls apart, add another egg. When the batter is just right, roll it into small balls and drop into the kettle. Cook, tightly covered, for 12 to 14 minutes. Do not remove the lid! Take up dumplings with slotted spoon, and serve with sour rabbit and gravy.

Also delicious with stewed chicken. Cook in the broth in which the chicken was stewed. *Makes 6 servings.*

HORN DISH

✳ Venison Ham

1 *fresh venison ham*
Marinade for Game (recipe
 follows)

salt
bacon fat
1 *to 1½ tablespoons cornstarch*

Marinate venison in an enamelware or glass dish in refrigerator for about 2 days, turning every 12 hours. Remove from marinade, wipe dry, season with salt, and brown well on all sides in bacon fat. Pour off excess fat and deglaze pan with ½ cup of marinade, strained. Return venison to pan, cover tightly, and bake in 350° oven for several hours, until well done. Time will vary according to size and age of animal. If necessary, add more marinade with equal amount of water during cooking, maintaining 1 to 1½ inches of liquid in bottom of pan. When done, remove meat to a hot platter. Thicken pan juices with cornstarch to serve with meat. Cranberry-Rice Stuffing or Brown Rice Pilau (see Index) go well with this hearty meat.

✳ Marinade for Game
(venison, duck, goose, or dove)

{ Adapted from "Mrs. S. A. Richmond's Venison Sauce," Grosvenor, 1850 }

1 onion, sliced	10 or 12 peppercorns
2 carrots, sliced	4 juniper berries, crushed
4 green onions, chopped	¼ teaspoon dried thyme
¼ cup chopped parsley	1 cup red wine
1 teaspoon salt	1 cup olive oil

Mix all ingredients to make a marinade. Marinate game in refrigerator for at least 12 hours, turning several times. Wipe game and proceed to cook as preferred. Venison (backstrap roast) is especially delicious when marinated in this mixture for 24 hours, then cooked over charcoal till just pink in the center. *Makes about 4 cups.*

PAUL REVERE SILVER
PORRINGER, 1795

✳❀✳ To Dress Ducks with Juice of Oranges

The ducks being singed, picked, and drawn, mince the livers with a little scraped bacon, some butter, green onions, sweet herbs and parsley, seasoned with salt, pepper, and mushrooms; these being all minced together, put them into the bodies of the ducks, and roast them, covered with slices of bacon, and wrapped up in paper; then put a little gravy, the juice of an orange, a few shallots minced, into a stew pan, and shake in a little pepper; when the ducks are roasted, take off the bacon, dish them, and pour your sauce with the juice of oranges over them, and serve them up hot.

The Virginia Housewife: or, Methodical Cook
Mrs. Mary Randolph, 1824

Dinner

✳ Stuffed Wild Goose or Wild Duck à l'Orange

{ Adapted from "To Dress Ducks with Juice of Oranges," The Virginia Housewife, 1824 }

Stuff 4 ducks or 2 geese with wild rice or half wild rice and half brown dressing. Stuff birds loosely. Place stuffed birds in a shallow pan, baste with orange sauce, and cover with foil. Cook in 300° oven for 1 hour. Uncover, baste again, and cook at 350° for 1 to 2 hours longer. Geese require longer time than ducks, and large ducks longer than teal. Baste often while the birds brown near the end, and test for tenderness. *Makes 5 or 6 servings.*

BROWN DRESSING
Fry ½ cup each of fine-chopped onion, celery and green pepper in butter or margarine until tender. Add 2 cups raw rice and brown mixture lightly. Add chopped poached livers and gizzards and moisten with the broth in which they have been cooked, adding more water if necessary. Season with salt, pepper, sage and poultry seasoning. The liquid must cover the rice. Cook slowly until the rice is dry.

ORANGE SAUCE
1 cup currant jelly, red or black
2 bay leaves
3 cups brown gravy (canned may be used)
juice of 4 oranges
grated rind of 2 oranges
grated rind of 1 lemon
6 to 8 whole peppercorns

Combine all ingredients in a saucepan; bring to a boil. Reduce heat and cook slowly for 20 minutes. Remove the bay leaves and peppercorns. Makes sufficient sauce for basting and serving with birds.

✳ Panbroiled Doves or Quails

This method is the best way to cook fresh game birds, but it does require constant attention.

The ingredients are the game birds, flour, salt, pepper, butter and oil, chicken stock and lemon juice. Allow 2 or 3 birds per person. Rub the birds with butter. Roll them in a mixture of flour, salt and pepper. Melt butter with a little oil in a deep heavy skillet. Over medium high heat, brown birds on all sides, turning often. Remove from skillet and set aside. Pour off excess butter and deglaze skillet with chicken stock, or chicken bouillon cube dissolved in water, and the juice of ½ lemon. Stir well to loosen all brown bits from the bottom of skillet. Return birds to skillet, cover, and allow to cook for 5 to 10 minutes longer, or until juices from the birds run clear. Remove birds to a hot platter and boil liquid rapidly until reduced to half. Ladle over birds and serve at once.

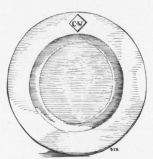

ENGLISH PEWTER
PLATE WITH CIPHER

✳ Stewed Quails, Squabs, or Cornish Game Hens

{ *Adapted from "To Stew Pigeons,"* Grosvenor, *1850* }

8 quails, or other small birds	*2 cups dry red wine*
salt and pepper	*2 tablespoons Cognac*
1 cup flour	*⅛ teaspoon dried thyme*
½ pound butter	*⅛ teaspoon dried tarragon*
½ cup chopped green onions with	*dash of grated nutmeg*
tops	*1 bay leaf*
1 can (2¼ ounces) deviled ham	*chopped parsley*
2 cups sliced mushrooms	

Rub birds inside and out with salt and pepper. Dredge well with flour. Melt 3 tablespoons butter in a skillet; brown birds, turning often. Remove from skillet. Melt 2 more tablespoons butter and sauté green onions until limp. Blend in deviled ham and mushrooms and cook for a few minutes. Remove from skillet and set aside. Melt remaining butter, add wine and

Cognac, and bring to a boil. Add thyme, tarragon, nutmeg and bay leaf. Stir well and return birds to skillet. Simmer, covered, until birds are tender, basting frequently. When birds are tender, remove to a heated platter and keep warm. Bring pan juices to boil and reduce to 1 cup. Remove bay leaf, stir in ham and mushroom mixture, and simmer for a few minutes. Correct seasonings, add parsley, and pour into a sauceboat to serve with the birds. Delicious as an accompaniment to the game. Serve with Cranberry-Rice Stuffing (see Index). *Makes 4 servings.*

❊ Birds in Wine

{ *Adapted from "To Stew Pigeons," Grosvenor, 1850* }

2 tablespoons brown sugar
2 cans (10½ ounces each)
   condensed beef bouillon
½ cup oil
½ cup soy sauce
2 teaspoons dried orégano or
   marjoram

1 garlic clove, minced
½ cup rosé wine
1 cup white Port wine
20 quails or doves
white pepper

This is the best way to cook game birds for a large crowd; the recipe can be expanded easily to cook as many birds as desired with the least amount of effort. Mix all ingredients except birds and pepper, to make a marinade, in a roasting pan with a cover. Arrange birds in the marinade, and pepper them. Do not add salt as other seasonings contain enough salt. Marinate for 3½ hours, or overnight. Cook in covered roaster in 375° oven for 2 hours. Check occasionally to see that there is always liquid in the pan, adding hot water as necessary. *Makes 6 servings.*

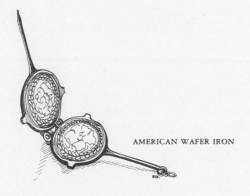

AMERICAN WAFER IRON

IRON SPIDER TRIVET

Chicken breasts were not tender enough in the old days to use as we do today. The recipes that follow use seasonings suggested by old recipes, but they are adapted to twentieth-century improved and tenderized birds.

A chicken breast is the whole breast portion of the bird. If the breast is to be split, boned or skinned, the recipe will so indicate.

✳ Cold Curried Chicken Breasts

{ *Adapted from "Chickens in Savoury Jelly,"* The Experienced English Housekeeper, *1794* }

8 medium-sized chicken breasts	*2 envelopes unflavored gelatin*
2 tablespoons onion salt	*¼ cup cold water*
2 tablespoons curry powder	*¼ cup heavy cream*
salt and white pepper	*pimiento strips*
2 cups strong chicken broth	*parsley sprigs*

In a shallow baking pan arrange chicken breasts bone side down. Sprinkle chicken with onion salt, curry powder, and salt and pepper to taste. Let stand, covered, in refrigerator overnight. Next day, turn skin side down, pour the broth over the pieces, and cover with foil. Make sure each breast is about half covered with broth. Poach in 350° oven for about 25 minutes, or until juices run clear. Do not overcook. Remove chicken to cool; skin may be removed at this point. Reserve the cooking broth. Soften gelatin in cold water, add to hot broth, and stir until dissolved. Correct seasonings. To ½ cup of the broth, add the heavy cream. Pour clear broth into a shallow pan and allow to set in refrigerator. Cool creamy broth until thick and almost set. Place chicken breasts on a serving platter, and glaze with creamy jelly. At serving time, cut clear chicken jelly into ½-inch cubes and arrange around breasts. Decorate with strips of pimiento and parsley bouquets. Serve cold with chutney. *Makes 8 servings.*

✳ Dijon Chicken

6 to 8 medium-sized chicken
    breasts, split, skinned and boned
1 cup hot water
2 teaspoons salt
4 to 6 tablespoons Dijon mustard

2 tablespoons butter or margarine
2 tablespoons flour
¼ cup heavy cream, approximately
white pepper

Place chicken breasts in a saucepan with hot water and 1½ teaspoons of the salt. Cover and simmer for about 10 minutes, or until almost tender. Remove chicken to a baking dish and save cooking liquid. Spread chicken with mustard. Make a roux with butter and flour; add ¾ cup of the reserved cooking liquid and ¼ cup cream. Stir over heat until the sauce is thick and creamy; flavor with white pepper and remaining ½ teaspoon salt. Pour sauce over chicken and bake in 350° oven for 12 to 15 minutes. Before serving, run under broiler to brown. *Makes 6 to 8 servings.*

SHEFFIELD SILVER-
PLATE PITCHER, 1775

✳ Chicken with Apples

4 medium-sized chicken breasts,
    boned, or enough chicken pieces
    for 4 people
2 teaspoons salt
4 tablespoons butter or margarine

⅔ cup apple juice or cider
1 tablespoon brandy or Calvados
½ teaspoon dried orégano
4 cooking apples, cored, quartered,
    and peeled

Rub chicken pieces with salt and brown in butter. Deglaze skillet with apple juice and brandy. Add rest of salt and the orégano, and return the chicken to skillet or to an ovenproof casserole. Cook, covered, in 350° oven for 25 to 30 minutes. Add apples about halfway through the cooking time. Remove chicken pieces and apples to a heated platter and keep warm. Pour pan juices into a skillet, or use the one in which chicken was browned. Cook over medium heat on top of the stove to reduce the juices to about 1/3 cup. Pour over chicken and apples. Serve with rice pilau. *Makes 4 servings.*

✳ Chicken Tahitian

4 large chicken breasts, split and
  skinned
5½ tablespoons plus 4 tablespoons
  butter
6 ounces frozen pineapple-orange
  juice concentrate
1 teaspoon ground ginger

1 teaspoon soy sauce
2 ounces (¼ cup) brandy
1 avocado, peeled and sliced
1 tablespoon lime juice
½ cup coarsely chopped Macadamia
  nuts

Brown chicken in 5½ tablespoons butter, and place in a shallow baking
dish. Heat frozen juice, ginger, soy sauce and 4 tablespoons butter; add
brandy when mix is hot. Brush over chicken. Bake in 350° oven for 35 to
40 minutes, basting frequently so that chicken is glazed and tender. Brush
avocado slices with lime juice and arrange chicken and avocado over rice
pilau, sprinkling Macadamia nuts over top. *Makes 4 to 6 servings.*

✳❊✳ *Shrimp Sauce*

Wash half a pint of shrimps very clean—mince and put them in
a stew-pan, with a spoonful of anchovy liquor, and a pound of
thick melted butter; boil it up for five minutes, and squeeze in
half a lemon. Toss it up, and put it in a sauce-boat.

The Virginia Housewife: or, Methodial Cook
Mrs. Mary Randolph, 1824

✳ Shrimp Sauce

{ *Adapted from "Shrimp Sauce,"* The Virginia
Housewife, 1824 }

½ pound butter
½ pound cleaned cooked shrimps,
  chopped fine

¼ teaspoon anchovy paste, or more
  to taste
squeeze of lemon juice

Melt butter in a saucepan. Add shrimps, anchovy paste and lemon juice. Heat thoroughly and serve with any broiled fish. *Makes about 2 cups.*

VARIATIONS

1 Try over scrambled eggs for a brunch or after-theater dish.

2 Use over tuna-fish croquettes.

3 Spoon over rice to which ½ teaspoon curry powder has been added.

4 Mix shrimps with 1 teaspoon anchovy paste, 2 cups sour cream and 1 teaspoon lemon juice. Pour over a crab-meat salad that has been heaped in avocado halves.

✳ Nancy's Barbecue Sauce
(for chickens, ribs, venison, brisket)

{ *Variation of "To Barbeque a Leg of Pork,"* The Experienced English Housekeeper, *1794* }

½ pound margarine
juice of 3 lemons
¼ cup fresh horseradish
¼ cup catsup

¼ cup white vinegar
1 tablespoon Worcestershire sauce
4 teaspoons salt
Tabasco

Combine all ingredients, using Tabasco to taste. Keep sauce warm and stir frequently as it tends to separate. Simmer for 1½ to 2 hours. *Makes about 3 cups, enough for barbecuing 4 half-chickens.*

✳ Caper Sauce
(for broiled fish)

{ *Adapted from "Caper Sauce,"* The Virginia Housewife, *1824* }

6 tablespoons butter
2 tablespoons flour
1 cup hot water
2 egg yolks (optional, but makes a richer sauce)

½ jar (2½-ounce jar) capers with caper vinegar
salt and pepper

In the top part of a double boiler, over boiling water, make a roux with 2 tablespoons of the butter and the flour; add hot water, and stir until smooth and creamy. Add beaten egg yolks slowly, having first warmed them with a little of the hot sauce. When well blended and thick, remove from heat and add remaining butter. Then add capers and vinegar. Taste to adjust seasonings. Use less of the caper vinegar for milder taste. *Makes about 2 cups.*

✳ Flavored Butters

CINNAMON BUTTER
3 tablespoons butter
1 teaspoon ground cinnamon

dash of cayenne pepper
squeeze of lemon juice

Work all ingredients together. Good with apple pancakes and acorn squash. *Makes ¼ cup.*

ORANGE BUTTER

{ *Adapted from "Fairy Butter,"*
The Art of Cookery, *1796* }

½ pound butter
½ pound confectioners' sugar

¼ cup frozen orange-juice concentrate

Cream all ingredients thoroughly. Store in a sealed container in refrigerator. Will last indefinitely. Serve on hot rolls. *Makes about 2 cups.*

HERB BUTTERS
4 tablespoons butter
squeeze of lemon juice

little white pepper (optional)
2 teaspoons chopped fresh herb

Use tarragon for fish or chicken; basil for grilled tomatoes; rosemary for lamb chops or chicken; mixed herbs for biscuits, toasted French bread, almost anything!

Cream all ingredients together, shape into a roll, wrap, and refrigerate. These butters, frozen, will keep the aroma of fresh herb for several months. *Makes ¼ cup.*

MUSTARD BUTTER
(for steaks, fish)
4 tablespoons butter
1 garlic clove, crushed

½ teaspoon dry mustard
1 teaspoon prepared Dijon mustard
few drops of white wine

TOMATO-ANCHOVY BUTTER
(for red snapper, cod, steaks)   1 teaspoon tomato paste
4 tablespoons butter   3 tablespoons anchovy paste
½ garlic clove, crushed   *paprika*

For mustard butter and tomato-anchovy butter, follow the same procedure as for herb butter. *Makes ¼ cup.*

✱ Stir-Fried Vegetables

5 to 6 tablespoons oil and melted   *salt*
*   butter, combined*   *½ cup chicken stock*
4 cups vegetables cut into small   *spices or seasonings as preferred*
*   slices (cauliflower, squash,*   *few drops of soy sauce (optional)*
*   carrots, celery, beets), or 6 cups*
*   greens (spinach torn into pieces,*
*   Chinese cabbage cut into thin*
*   slices across the stalk, Swiss*
*   chard)*

In a large heavy skillet or wok, heat the oil and butter. When hot but not smoking, add vegetables and stir-fry for about 2 minutes, stirring constantly so as not to burn the vegetables. Turn heat to medium and add salt to taste, stock and preferred seasonings. Cover tightly and continue cooking for 5 to 8 minutes for root or hard vegetables, about 2 minutes for greens. Serve immediately. *Makes 6 servings.*

SEASONINGS
   All vegetables: chopped green onions
   Cauliflower: crushed coriander seeds
   Carrots: dillweed
   Squash: orégano
   Beets: little sugar and ginger
   Celery: crushed aniseed

COPPER AND WOOD
BERRY SCOOP

✻ Basic Vegetable Soufflé

3 eggs, separated
1 cup very thick cream sauce
2 cups seasoned cooked vegetables,
  chopped very fine

salt and pepper
desired herb or spice

Beat egg yolks well. Add to cream sauce and vegetables. Taste for seasonings. Beat egg whites stiff and gently fold into vegetable mixture. Pour into a well-oiled 4-cup soufflé dish, scooped-out tomato halves, or individual cocottes. Set dishes in a warm-water bath (1½ inches of water), tomatoes in a flat pan that can be set in a larger pan of water. Bake in 350° oven for about 1 hour for large soufflé and less time for smaller dishes. Watch tomatoes and small dishes after about 15 to 20 minutes. Test for doneness with a knife; it will come out clean when soufflé is baked. *Makes 4 to 6 servings.*

STIEGEL-TYPE GLASS TUMBLER,
PENNSYLVANIA, 1772

✻ Barley

This often neglected grain is a delicious accompaniment to game birds or roast beef.

Pearl barley: rinse in a colander, then cover with cold water and add 1 teaspoon salt for 1 cup barley. Bring to a boil, reduce heat to a simmer, and cook for about 1 hour, or until tender. You may need to skim off the top occasionally as the barley cooks. Stir now and then to keep from sticking on the bottom.

Scotch barley: soak in cold water to cover overnight. Drain, cover with fresh cold water, then proceed as with pearl barley.

Season with salt, pepper and butter. Sliced mushrooms and chopped green onions browned in butter make a delicious addition mixed with the cooked barley.

✳ Spinach Rice

2 eggs
⅓ cup milk
½ teaspoon dried thyme
½ teaspoon dried rosemary
½ teaspoon Worcestershire sauce
salt and pepper

1 cup shredded sharp cheese
1 cup cooked rice
½ cup fine-chopped onion
1 package (10 ounces) frozen
   chopped spinach, thawed
2 tablespoons butter

Beat eggs; add milk, herbs, Worcestershire, and salt and pepper to taste. Stir in cheese, rice, onion and drained spinach. Pour into an oiled 4-cup casserole and dot top with butter. Bake in 350° oven until mixture bubbles and is cooked through. *Makes 6 servings.*

✳ Cranberry-Rice Stuffing

1 package (6 ounces) long-grain
   and wild-rice mix
1 cup fresh cranberries
1 cup thin-sliced celery

¼ cup sugar
1 teaspoon grated orange rind
⅓ cup chopped green onions

Cook rice with its seasonings according to package directions. Add cranberries and heat till they begin to pop. Stir in rest of ingredients. Mix well and spoon into an oiled 4-cup casserole. Cover and bake in 350° oven for 30 to 40 minutes. Good with all poultry and ham. Excellent accompaniment to wild game birds. *Makes 6 servings.*

✳ Brown Rice Pilau

1½ cups raw brown rice
3 cups chicken stock
1 teaspoon ground turmeric
⅓ cup dried currants
¼ cup Madeira wine

½ cup chopped green onions
⅓ cup pine nuts
1½ tablespoons minced preserved
   gingerroot
2 tablespoons butter

Cook rice in chicken stock with turmeric till done, about 45 minutes. Remove from heat and add rest of ingredients. Let stand over hot water for 15 minutes before serving. Fine with chicken, turkey and ham. *Makes 6 servings.*

✳ Cheese-Jalapeño Grits

1½ cups grits (see Note)
½ tablespoon salt
6 cups boiling water
¼ pound butter
1 pound sharp cheese, grated
1 tablespoon seasoned salt

3 eggs
2 jalapeño peppers, seeded and
   chopped fine, or 1 can (4
   ounces) chopped green chilies
2 tablespoons finely chopped
   pimiento

Cook grits and salt in boiling water for about 5 minutes. Add butter, grated cheese and seasoned salt, mixing well; cool. Beat eggs and stir into the cooled grits mixture. Add jalapeños or chilies, a little at a time until the desired "hotness" is reached; add pimientos. Spoon into a greased 2-quart casserole and cook, covered, in 350° oven for about 45 minutes.

This is equally good without the jalapeños or chilies. *Makes 8 servings.*

NOTE
Grits, or hominy grits, are coarsely ground hulled dried corn kernels. Grits are widely used as a starchy vegetable in the South and Southwest.

✳ Potato Croquettes

{ *Adapted from "Potato Balls,"* The Virginia Housewife, 1824 }

4 cups seasoned mashed potatoes
2 eggs, separated

salt and pepper
1½ cups fine bread crumbs

Mix mashed potatoes while still warm with beaten egg yolks, and salt and pepper to taste. Form into balls and dip into the slightly beaten egg whites. Roll in bread crumbs and deep-fry at about 385° till brown. *Makes 24 to 30 small or 16 large croquettes.*

VARIATIONS
1 Add ½ cup shredded cheese to hot potato mix. Proceed as above.

2 Season the mixture with ½ teaspoon onion salt and 1 tablespoon grated Parmesan cheese. Roll the balls in crushed cornflakes and place in a buttered casserole. Bake in 350° oven till brown.

3 Add ½ cup fine-chopped parsley and 1 tablespoon fine-chopped green onion to mixture. Roll balls in crushed crisp bacon bits, and bake in 350° oven till heated through.

✳·❀·✳ Egg Plants, Stuffed

Parboil them to take off their bitterness. Then slit each one down the side, and extract the seeds. Have ready a stuffing made of grated bread-crumbs, butter, minced sweet herbs, salt, pepper, nutmeg, and beaten yolk of egg. Fill with it the cavity from whence you took the seeds, and bake the egg plants in a Dutch oven. Serve them up with a made gravy poured into the dish.

Directions for Cookery, In Its Various Branches
Miss Leslie, 1839

✳ Stuffed Eggplant

{ *Adapted from "Egg Plants, Stuffed,"* Miss Leslie's Directions for Cookery, *1839* }

1 large eggplant	*1 tablespoon chopped parsley*
1 cup soft bread crumbs	*salt and pepper*
1 large onion, chopped fine	*¼ teaspoon ground marjoram or*
1 small green pepper, chopped fine	*orégano, approximately*
1 celery rib, chopped fine	*1 egg, well beaten*
1 tablespoon bacon drippings	*buttered bread crumbs for topping*

Parboil eggplant in salted water for 10 minutes. Cut into halves; remove pulp. Reserve the shells, and drain and chop the pulp. Mix 1½ cups chopped pulp and bread crumbs together lightly. Sauté onion, green pepper and celery in bacon drippings. Add to eggplant and crumb mixture together with parsley, salt and pepper to taste, marjoram or orégano to taste, and beaten egg. Fill the eggplant shells with this mixture and top with buttered bread crumbs. Bake at 350° for 30 minutes, with 2 tablespoons water in the pan to keep the shells moist. *Makes 4 servings.*

VARIATIONS
1 Add about ½ cup sautéed chopped mushrooms to filling.
2 Add 4 ounces canned tomatoes, drained and chopped, to filling. Season with basil, orégano and garlic salt. Add grated Parmesan cheese to the buttered crumb topping.
3 Brown ½ to 2/3 pound ground meat, stirring to keep it in small pieces during browning. Add to any of the fillings and bake.

✳ Zucchini-Eggplant Bake

2 pounds zucchini
1 large eggplant
1 egg
1½ pounds cream cheese, softened
1 can (4 ounces) chopped green
   chilies

salt and pepper
garlic salt
1½ cups buttered bread crumbs
½ teaspoon dried orégano

Wash zucchini, do not peel, and cut into thin slices. Peel and cube egg-plant. Parboil in salted water for a few minutes and drain well. In a well-oiled baking dish put a layer of raw zucchini and a layer of eggplant, al-ternating until dish is full. Beat egg; add softened cream cheese, chilies, and salt, pepper and garlic salt to taste. Pour over vegetables. Top with buttered bread crumbs mixed with orégano. Bake in 350° oven for 30 to 45 minutes. (Freezes well, before final cooking.) *Makes 6 to 8 servings.*

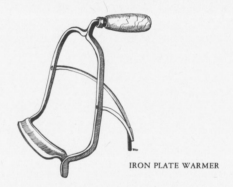

IRON PLATE WARMER

✳ Apple-Stuffed Acorn Squash

2 acorn squashes, about 1 pound
   each
2 tart cooking apples
1 tablespoon fresh lemon juice

½ tablespoon grated lemon rind
⅓ cup packed brown sugar
4 tablespoons butter or margarine
salt and ground cinnamon

Cut squashes into halves. Place in a shallow baking dish, cut side down, and add ½ inch of water. Bake in 375° oven for about 35 minutes, or until almost tender. Do not allow to boil dry. Pour off water, and scoop out seeds. Make apple filling: core, peel, and dice apples and mix them with the lemon juice, grated lemon rind and brown sugar. Mix about 2 ta-blespoons of the butter with this filling. Use remaining butter to brush over the cooked squash halves. Sprinkle squashes with salt and cinnamon, fill the halves with the apple mixture, and place in a baking dish. Add ½ inch of boiling water, cover pan tightly, and bake for 30 minutes. Before serving, pour pan juices over the squashes. *Makes 4 servings.*

VARIATION

2 acorn squashes   4 teaspoons butter
salt   4 tablespoons dry sherry
pinch of onion salt (optional)

Cook squashes as in basic recipe. Sprinkle with salt and onion salt. Add 1 teaspoon butter and 1 tablespoon sherry to each squash "cup" and return to oven. Bake at 350° until butter melts and is absorbed by the squash. Baste squashes with the sherry-butter mixture during this last cooking.

❋ Creamy Summer Squash

{ *Adapted from "Squash or Cimlin,"* The Virginia Housewife, *1824* }

2½ pounds yellow squash   ¼ cup coarse bread crumbs
½ teaspoon salt   salt and pepper
1 small onion, chopped   ⅓ cup grated Parmesan cheese
2 tablespoons butter   ⅓ cup fine dry bread crumbs
¾ cup heavy cream or sour cream

Cut squashes into pieces and cook in salted water until done. Drain and mash. Sauté onion in butter and add to squash. Add cream, coarse bread crumbs, and salt and pepper to taste. Pour into a buttered 4-cup casserole and cover with a topping made of mixed cheese and fine crumbs. Bake in 350° oven for 30 minutes, or until top is golden brown. *Makes 6 servings.*

❋ Scalloped Tomatoes

{ *Adapted from "To Scollop Tomatoes,"* The Virginia Housewife, *1824* }

Oil a casserole of desired size. Peel and slice ripe firm tomatoes. Layer tomatoes, small amount of bread crumbs, salt, pepper, fine-chopped green onions. Sprinkle each layer with chopped fresh dill or basil; dot with butter and sour cream. Continue layers, ending with bread crumbs, butter and sour cream. Bake in 325° oven for 25 to 30 minutes, or until tomatoes are soft but not too mushy. This idea has possibilities for many variations as to seasonings, and the basic recipe can be adjusted for desired number of servings.

VARIATIONS

1 Add grated Parmesan cheese to bread crumbs with a pinch of marjoram or orégano, chopped green onions and garlic salt. Dot with butter only, omitting sour cream.

2 Use rye bread crumbs, crushed seasoned crackers, French bread with sesame seeds, for different flavorings.

3 Slice tomatoes, season with salt and pepper, cover with sour cream, sprinkle with curry powder, and top with buttered crumbs.

✳ Sweet Potato Pudding

{ *Variation of "Sweet Potato Pudding,"* The Virginia Housewife, *1824* }

2 eggs	*½ teaspoon grated nutmeg*
¾ cup sugar	*½ teaspoon grated lemon rind*
2½ cups grated sweet potatoes	*¼ cup sherry*
4 tablespoons butter	*pinch of salt*
1 cup milk	*butter for top*

Beat eggs and sugar until creamy. Add rest of ingredients and pour into buttered 6-cup baking dish. Cook in 350° oven for about 45 minutes, stirring occasionally. When liquid is absorbed and potatoes are done, brown top under broiler with a few dots of butter. Good with ham, turkey, duck or goose. *Makes 6 servings.*

✳ Yams 'n' Carrots

4 medium-sized yams, cooked and sliced	*¾ teaspoon salt*
	¾ cup corn syrup
1 pound carrots, cooked and sliced	*grated rind of 1 small orange*
1 cup pitted prunes	*¾ cup orange juice*
2 tablespoons cornstarch	

Combine yams, carrots and prunes in a 2-quart baking dish. Combine rest of ingredients and pour over the dish. Bake in 350° oven for 40 to 45 minutes, basting frequently. *Makes 6 servings.*

EARLY AMERICAN BOTTLE
WITH WITCH'S BALL STOPPER

✳ Beets in Orange Sauce

2 cans (16 ounces each) small
   whole beets
4 tablespoons butter
1 cup orange juice
3 tablespoons sugar

grated rind of 1 lemon
juice of ½ lemon
⅓ teaspoon salt
1 teaspoon vinegar
⅓ cup cornstarch

Drain beets, reserving liquid, and put them in a saucepan with the butter over low heat. Pour in orange juice, sugar and lemon rind. Mix lemon juice, salt, vinegar and cornstarch with ½ cup beet liquid until smooth. Add to beets. Heat through, stirring constantly. Taste, and adjust salt if necessary. *Makes 6 to 8 servings.*

✳✳ *To ragoo Cucumbers.*

Take two cucumbers and two onions, slice them and fry them in a little butter, then drain them in a sieve; put them into a saucepan, add six spoonfuls of gravy, two of white wine, a blade of mace; let them stew five or six minutes; then take a piece of butter as big as a walnut, rolled in flour, a little salt and Cayenne pepper; shake them together, and when it is thick, dish them up.

The Art of Cookery Made Plain and Easy
Hannah Glasse, 1796

✳ Poached Cucumbers

{ *Adapted from "To Ragoo Cucumbers,"* The Art of Cookery, *1796* }

6 medium-sized cucumbers (about
   3 pounds)
½ tablespoon salt
2 tablespoons butter
½ cup chopped onion
2 tablespoons flour

2 cups milk
2 tablespoons (or more) sour cream
1 tablespoon chopped fresh dill, or
   1 teaspoon dried dill
parsley sprigs

Peel and seed cucumbers and cut into 1-inch pieces. Sprinkle with salt and let stand for about 15 minutes. Place in a colander to allow liquid to drain thoroughly. Melt butter in a heavy skillet and sauté the onion until pale gold. Add flour, stirring constantly. Pour in milk, bring to a boiling point, and reduce heat to simmer for about 2 minutes, until mixture thickens a little. Add cucumbers and simmer until they are just tender. Add sour cream and dill, adjust seasonings, and garnish with fresh parsley sprigs. Good with chicken and fish. *Makes 6 servings.*

✳ Celery Chablis

{ *Adapted from "To Stew Celery,"* The Experienced English Housekeeper, *1794* }

1 stalk of celery
½ cup water
½ cup Chablis wine
salt
3 tablespoons butter

3 tablespoons flour
¾ cup chicken stock
white pepper
Parmesan cheese
paprika

Separate stalk of celery into ribs. Cut ribs into 2-inch lengths. Poach in a mixture of the water and Chablis with a little salt. Remove with a slotted spoon when almost done; reserve cooking liquid. Place celery in an oiled 4-cup casserole. Melt butter in top part of double boiler over boiling water. Add flour to make a light roux. Stir in chicken stock and ½ cup of the reserved cooking liquid, and stir until sauce is thick. Season with salt and white pepper to taste. Pour over celery; sprinkle top with Parmesan cheese and a little paprika. Bake in 400° oven for about 20 minutes. *Makes 6 servings.*

✳ *To pickle Gerkins another Way*

Wipe your small gerkins with a dry cloth, then make a pickle of vinegar, salt, whole pepper, cloves, and mace, boil it, and pour it on hot; set the jar in an oven almost cold for three or four different days till the cucumbers are green; when cold cover them close.

N.B. You must cover the gerkins with a linen cloth and a plate while they are doing to keep in the steam.

The Art of Cookery Made Plain and Easy
Hannah Glasse, 1796

✳ Dilly Carrots
(or okra, green beans, cauliflower)

{ *Adapted from "To Pickle Gerkins Another Way,"*
The Art of Cookery, 1796 }

4 cups vinegar
1 cup water
½ cup salt
4 or 5 garlic cloves

4 or 5 small hot peppers
4 or 5 stems of fresh dill, or 2½
teaspoons whole pickling spice

Prepare a sufficient quantity of desired vegetable to pack tightly into the pint jars. Carrots should be peeled and sliced lengthwise into strips; okra should be washed and stems trimmed; green beans cut into uniform-size pieces; and cauliflower cut into uniform-size flowerets.

Boil together the vinegar, water and salt. Pack vegetables, 1 garlic clove, 1 hot pepper and 1 stem of dill in each sterilized jar. Pour the vinegar mixture over the vegetables, and seal jars. These should stand for 3 or 4 weeks before using. (When using whole pickling spice, put ½ teaspoon in each jar.) *Makes 4 or 5 pints.*

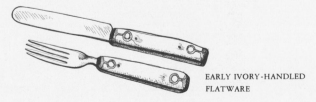

EARLY IVORY-HANDLED
FLATWARE

✳ Bread and Butter Pickles

25 medium-sized cucumbers
3 onions, sliced thin
½ cup salt
1 quart vinegar
2 cups sugar

2 tablespoons each of mustard
seeds, celery seeds and ground
ginger
1 tablespoon ground tumeric

Soak clean whole cucumbers in cold water overnight. Next day, slice, un-peeled, very thin. Add sliced onions, cover with salt, and let stand for 1 hour. Combine vinegar, sugar and spices in a saucepan. Bring to boil. Drain cucumbers and onions, add to vinegar, and cook for 3 minutes. Pour into hot sterilized jars and seal at once. *Makes about 6 pints.*

✳ Pickled Peaches, Pears, Figs, or Plums

{ *Adapted from* The Art of Cookery, *1796* }

4 pounds peaches or other fruit
½ ounce whole allspice
½ ounce whole cloves

½ ounce cinnamon sticks
3 pounds sugar
2 cups white vinegar

Prepare fruits; wash well, and peel pears or peaches. Tie spices in a cheese-cloth bag. In a large kettle, combine sugar and vinegar. Bring to a boil and add the spice bag. Boil for 10 minutes, then remove the spices. Skim syrup. Add fruits and cook until tender. Remove from syrup with a slotted spoon and pack into sterile jars. Put ½ cinnamon stick in each jar if desired. Cook liquid until thick and syrupy. Pour over fruits in jars and seal immediately. *Makes 3 pints.*

ENGLISH SILVER
WINE CADDY, 1790

✳ Jalapeño Jelly

{ Traditional Mexican }

1 cup fine-chopped green pepper
¼ cup fine-chopped jalapeños (wear
  rubber gloves)
6 cups sugar
2 tablespoons cider vinegar

1 tablespoon salt
1 bottle (6 ounces) liquid fruit
  pectin
green food coloring

Mix all ingredients except bottled pectin and coloring and boil for 4 minutes. Cool for 1 minute. Add pectin and a little green food coloring. Pour into hot sterilized jars and seal. *Makes about 5½ pints.*

CONTINENTAL TUREEN
WITH TOWLE LID

✳ Fresh Prune Chutney

(or pear or peach or green tomato)

*{ Variation of "To Make Paco-lilla, or Indian
Pickle . . . ," The Art of Cookery, 1796}*

1 cup brown sugar
1 cup granulated sugar
¾ cup vinegar
½ tablespoon crushed hot red
  peppers
2 teaspoons salt
2 teaspoons mustard seeds

3 garlic cloves, sliced
¼ onion, sliced
½ cup sliced crystallized gingerroot
1 cup raisins
3½ cups sliced fresh prunes
1 lemon, rind and all, ground

Combine all ingredients in a deep large kettle. (When using green tomatoes add 1 additional cup of granulated sugar.) Simmer over low heat for several hours, until thick and brown. Bottle in hot sterilized jars and seal. *Makes about 4 pints.*

✳ Basic Pastry

{ Adapted from "To Make a Paste for This Pie," The Virginia Housewife, 1824 }

2 cups all-purpose flour　　*5½ tablespoons cold butter*
½ teaspoon salt　　　　　*⅓ cup shortening*
½ teaspoon sugar　　　　 *5 tablespoons cold water*

Sift flour twice, adding salt and sugar to the second sifting. With a pastry blender, cut in the cold butter and shortening. Add water and blend lightly. For recipes calling for precooked pastry bottoms, roll out half of the dough between 2 pieces of wax paper. Transfer to pan and trim edges. Cover with buttered foil and weight with beans or a glass dish that just fits inside, so that the pastry will not rise. Bake at 400° for 9 minutes; remove foil, and prick bottom. Bake for 3 or 4 minutes more, until edges begin to brown lightly. Use remaining half for top crust, or refrigerate and use later for another pie. *Makes enough for 2-crust 9-inch pie.*

✳ Sour-Cream Pastry

{ Adapted from "To Make Puff Paste," The Virginia Housewife, 1824 }

6 tablespoons butter　　　　*⅓ cup sour cream*
¾ cup flour

Cut butter into flour until mealy. Stir in sour cream. Wrap in wax paper and refrigerate for 8 or more hours. Roll out and fit into ungreased pie tin or 4 to 6 tart pans. Bake in 350° oven for 15 minutes, or until brown.

Can also be used for shortcake. Bake on an ungreased cookie sheet. *Makes enough for 1-crust 9-inch pie.*

AUBERGINE LUSTRE PITCHER

✳ Crumb Pie Shells

1½ cups crushed cookie crumbs   *⅓ cup melted butter*

Combine crumbs and butter and press firmly into pie pan. Bake in 350°
oven for 8 to 10 minutes; do not brown. Cool and fill with desired filling.
   Types of crumbs that can be used:
      chocolate cookies (fill with peppermint ice cream topped with choco-
      late sauce).
      ginger cookies (fill with spiced pumpkin custard).
      various presweetened dry cereals (fill with lemon custard).

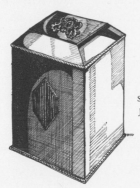

SHEFFIELD BISQUIT BOX,
J. GREEN, MAKER

✳ Meringue Shells

{ *Adapted from "Peppermint Drops,"* A New System of
Domestic Cookery, 1807 }

1 teaspoon water   *1 cup sugar*
1 teaspoon white vinegar *½ teaspoon baking powder*
1 teaspoon vanilla extract *½ teaspoon salt*
3 egg whites

Add the water, vanilla, and vinegar to egg whites. Whip them stiff, then
very slowly add sugar, baking powder and salt mixed together. Shape
meringue shells or pie shell on a cookie sheet that has been covered with
aluminum foil. Bake in 275° oven for 1 hour. Turn off oven at this point
and allow meringues to cool completely in the oven. Serve filled with fresh
strawberries, sugared, and covered with whipped cream slightly sweetened.
Or fill with a good tart lemon curd and whipped cream. Or fill with rich
vanilla or chocolate ice cream and pour chocolate sauce over all. *Makes 8
small shells or one 9-inch pie shell.*

✻ Lemon Curd Tarts

{ Adapted from "Lemon Cream," The Experienced English Housekeeper, 1794 }

3 eggs
2 tablespoons grated lemon rind
6 tablespoons lemon juice
⅛ teaspoon salt

¾ cup sugar
⅜ pound butter, softened
4 to 6 baked tart shells

Beat the eggs in the top part of a double boiler. Add remaining ingredients. Stir over hot water until thick. Chill. Fill tart shells just before serving. Garnish with a small dollop of whipped cream and candied violets if desired.

This filling is also delicious served in a meringue shell, topped with whipped cream flavored with ¼ teaspoon of vanilla extract.

✻ Southern Lemon Chess Pie

{ Variation of "A Second Lemon Cream," The Art of Cookery, 1796}

2 cups sugar
¼ pound butter or margarine
6 eggs, well beaten
½ cup lemon juice

grated rind of ½ lemon
1 heaping tablespoon cornmeal
pastry for 1-crust 9-inch pie

Cream the sugar and butter. Add the beaten eggs, then lemon juice and rind, and cornmeal. Pour into a 9-inch pie tin lined with unbaked pastry, and bake at 400° for 15 minutes. Reduce heat to 375° and continue baking for about 30 minutes longer, or until lightly browned. *Makes 6 servings.*

✻ Southern Pecan Pie

2 eggs, well beaten
1 cup dark corn syrup
⅛ teaspoon salt
2 teaspoons vanilla extract

1 cup sugar
3 tablespoons melted butter
1 cup pecan halves
pastry for 1-crust 9-inch pie

Mix all ingredients except pastry, and pour into a 9-inch pie tin lined with the unbaked pastry. Bake in 400° oven for about 40 minutes, or until a knife inserted in the center comes out clean. Serve with vanilla ice cream or whipped cream. *Makes 8 servings.*

✳☙✳ The Experienced English Housekeeper *includes a chapter with general directions on making sweet pies. The following is Mrs. Raffald's receipt for "icing" or meringue:*

"BEAT the white of an egg to a strong froth, put in by degrees four ounces of double-refined sugar, with as much gum as will lie on a sixpence, beat and sifted fine, beat it half an hour, then lay it over your tarts the thickness of a straw."

The Experienced English Housekeeper
Elizabeth Raffald, 1794

✳ "Unexpected Guests" Quick Apple Pie

{ *Adapted from "Malborough Pudding,"* Grosvenor, *1850* }

5½ cups cooking apples (sweet McIntosh are wonderful for this)
1 tablespoon lemon juice
1 teaspoon vanilla extract
½ cup packed brown sugar (⅔ cup if apples are tart)
2 tablespoons cornstarch
⅛ teaspoon salt
½ teaspoon ground cinnamon
⅛ teaspoon grated nutmeg
½ teaspoon grated lemon rind
2 tablespoons butter
pastry for 1-crust 8-inch pie

Peel and core the apples, and cut into thin slices. Toss lemon juice over apples; add vanilla. Mix dry ingredients together and sift over apples. Add lemon rind and toss until thoroughly blended. Butter a 7- or 8-inch pie tin. Arrange apples in the tin, heaping them up at the center to make a small mound. Dot with butter. Roll out dough and cut into strips. Arrange strips in lattice fashion over the apples. Bake in preheated 350° oven for 30 to 40 minutes, or till crust is golden brown. *Makes 6 servings.*

Orange Meringue Pie

CRUNCHY COCOA CRUST

⅓ cup powdered cocoa mix *1 ⅓ cups sifted flour*
½ cup shortening *½ teaspoon salt*
¼ cup boiling water

Combine cocoa mix and shortening. Add boiling water, then sifted flour and salt. Mix quickly and form into ball. Roll out between 2 sheets of wax paper and fit into 9-inch pie tin. Prick bottom and sides. Bake in 425° oven for 15 minutes. Cool.

ORANGE FILLING

4 eggs, separated *grated rind of ½ orange*
1 cup sugar *grated rind of ½ lemon*
3 tablespoons flour *¼ teaspoon grated nutmeg*
1 cup orange juice *2 tablespoons butter*
juice of ½ lemon

Beat egg yolks and sugar together in the top part of a double boiler. Add flour, then juices, rinds and nutmeg. Place over hot water, and stir with a wooden spoon until thick, approximately 10 minutes. Remove from heat and stir in butter. Cool slightly and put on the cooled cocoa pie shell.

MERINGUE TOPPING

4 egg whites *4 tablespoons sugar*
¼ teaspoon cream of tartar *½ teaspoon vanilla extract*

Beat egg whites frothy, then add cream of tartar. Continue to beat, adding sugar 1 tablespoon at a time. Then add vanilla. Do not beat too stiff. Place on top of orange filling in pie tin, covering to edge of crust. Bake in preheated 400° oven for 7 to 10 minutes, or until peaks turn light brown. *Makes 6 servings.*

VARIATION

Instead of meringue for a topping, try sweetened whipped cream, then sprinkle shaved unsweetened chocolate on top.

✳ Key Lime Pie

{ Variation of "A Second Lemon Cream," The Art of Cookery, 1796 }

1 tall can (14 ounces) sweetened
  condensed milk
½ cup lime juice
3 eggs, separated, at room
  temperature

pinch of salt
green food coloring
9-inch baked pie shell

Chill condensed milk in refrigerator overnight. Place in a large mixing bowl and beat at high speed for several minutes. Add lime juice, a few drops at a time, scraping sides; mixture will thicken. Add egg yolks, one at a time, and continue beating. Beat egg whites until stiff and fold into mixture gently. Add a few grains of salt. Last, add a few drops of green food coloring. Pour immediately into the pie shell, and chill in refrigerator for several hours before serving. *Makes 6 servings.*

NOTE
A baked pastry piecrust is better than a graham-cracker crust for this pie because the graham-cracker crust is too sweet, spoiling the tartness of the lime taste.

ENGLISH BRASS
PASTRY JIGGER/CRIMP

✳ Pumpkin Chiffon Pie

{ Variation of "Pumpkin Pudding," American Cookery, 1796 }

3 eggs, separated
1 cup sugar
½ teaspoon salt
½ teaspoon grated mace
1 teaspoon vanilla extract
2 envelopes unflavored gelatin
½ cup cold milk

1 cup milk, scalded
2 cups mashed cooked pumpkin
9-inch baked pie shell made with
  ginger cookie crumbs
ginger cookie crumbs, browned in
  butter

Beat egg yolks and add sugar, salt, mace and vanilla. Mix thoroughly. Soften gelatin in cold milk. Add egg-sugar mixture, a little at a time, to the scalded milk, stirring constantly. Cook over low heat until thick. Stir in softened gelatin, blend, and add pumpkin. Place in refrigerator till *almost* set. Beat egg whites stiff and fold into cold pumpkin mix. Turn into the crumb pie shell and sprinkle the browned ginger cookie crumbs over the top. Refrigerate until set. *Makes 6 to 8 servings.*

VARIATION

Pumpkin mousse: Whip 1 cup of heavy cream to soft-peak stage. Fold into chiffon-pumpkin filling, and turn into 6-cup soufflé dish with a paper collar to set. Garnish with finely chopped crystallized gingerroot. *Makes 8 servings.*

SALT-GLAZE SOUTHERN STONEWARE
PRESERVE JAR WITH RAG STOPPER

Supper and Tea

Supper! What is there to say about a meal that probably did not even exist for many settlers during the early days of the Colonies and later seemed more like a bedtime snack made up of leftovers? At a much later date as the western movement spread, Frederick Law Olmsted records in his diary of travels through Texas in 1853-1854, ". . . on our supper table was nothing else than the eternal fry, pone, and coffee . . ." The eternal fry was the inevitable salt pork or occasionally beef.

In the eighteenth century supper was a brief meal and, especially in the South, light and late. It generally consisted of leftovers from dinner, or of gruel (a mixture made from boiling water with oats, "Indian," or some other meal). One Massachusetts diary of 1797 describes roast potatoes, prepared with salt but no butter. Ale, cider, or some variety of beer was always served.

In the richer merchant society and in Southern plantation life, eggs and egg dishes were special delicacies and were prepared as side dishes at either dinner or supper. A favorite was egg salmagundi, hard-cooked eggs served with a variety of leftover meats, vegetables and nuts. Eggs that were laid on Christmas day were believed by Dutch settlers to reduce a hernia. Salads in season were prepared much as they are today. Various pickles and soups often appeared for supper. Most leftover fish and meats were reserved for hashes and pasties which could be served for breakfast the next day. Bread, and sometimes butter, and a sweet dish, usually fruit, completed the meal.

One journal describes artichokes, huckleberries and milk on one occasion, and coffee, bread and butter on another. Dr. Alexander Hamilton's *Itinerarium*, written in 1744, records "cold gammon" and salad at one supper and "pickled oysters" (these seem to have been a great favorite at all meals) at another.

One remarkable journal, heretofore unpublished, sheds light on the customs of Philadelphians in the early nineteenth century. It was written by Emma Newbold Janvier, born in 1811. She was an educated, perceptive and articulate woman writing to her son Thomas Janvier (an author of some note) describing her life as a young girl. ". . . some families always served a 10 o'clock supper of cold meats, etc." In winter her father frequently had a few friends to late suppers of terrapin or roasted oysters. The oysters would be laid on hickory coals in the dining-room fireplace and brought on a pewter platter to the table by a servant carrying them in fresh relays. "The table was neatly set with pewter plates and regular buck-handled oyster knives, with a crash towel for each guest . . ." ". . . the oysters were relishing with plenty of choice Philadelphia butter and good bread (from Fraley's celebrated bakery)." What cozy, intimate gatherings these must have been!

Mrs. Janvier remembers with delight the custom of "odd-times" eating. In the back parlor of Mrs. Janvier's grandmother's home, there was a double-doored closet or pantry which adjoined the chimney and extended under the stairs. Here were found, along with fine china and silver, "dainties for odd-times eating." These included mince pie or potato pudding left over from dessert, rich cake in a black earthen jar, "her Queen cake and 'dried rusk' and Bunns." "The atmosphere in that closet had a perfume composed of mingled pies, cheese, cake, wine, walnut, pickles, and, in winter, apples, chiefly 'Bellflower.' Children remember such closets long after childhood is past. I can inhale the odor of that one yet, whenever I want to, in memory."

Apples roasted on a string before a blazing fire in the evening were another delight described by Mrs. Janvier. A dish was placed beneath the apples to collect the sweet juices as the apples twirled and dripped before the fire. Her father, provided with a decanter of brandy, hot water and sugar, mixed these ingredients with the apple juices and had "his Apple Toddy." Mrs. Janvier goes on to comment, "I wonder if this old fashioned beverage is ever made in these days of *efforts* after Temperance?"

The custom of serving tea was popular during the eighteenth century when tea became *the* social drink. When it was first introduced, Colonists, not understanding its use, stewed the leaves in butter, threw out what liq-

SHEFFIELD SILVER TEAPOT,
ENGLISH, 1770

uid collected and munched on the leaves. Later, when the practice of drinking tea was understood, the leaves were highly valued and were used over and over. The term "brewing" tea came from the English expression for "brewing" beer. As a result of high prices and the tea strike, tea was labeled dangerous and was thought to cause deadly diseases. In time, coffee became the favorite American drink and tea survived primarily as a medicine, quite a change from the early "Revolutionary" claims! Colonists invented their own types of coffee, grinding it from such diverse items as roasted nuts and roots.

Teatime provided a quiet little hour for refinement and gossip. Dr. Hamilton happily recalls taking tea with a Mrs. Cume at 5 o'clock, "There was a lady with her who gave us an elegant dish of scandal to relish our tea." Eighteenth-century Colonials enjoyed their "dish of tea" in the parlor. On the tea table, which did not have a cloth for teatime, would stand the teapot, slop bowl, a milk pitcher or creamer, tea canister, sugar container, tongs, teacups, saucers and spoons. The "china" would have most likely been salt glaze or, for the very rich, porcelain. The teapot could well have been silver. A brass teakettle containing boiling water was placed on a lampstand close to the tea table. Thin slices of bread and butter or little sweet buns were offered, and occasionally coffee was also served. For a short time in Colonial history, high tea was fashionable and took the place of supper in a few wealthy homes. This, however, was never a popular custom.

Supper took on added importance as the nineteenth century wore on. This heretofore casual meal became more important as dinner was served earlier in the day. Many rural farming communities today continue to have mealtime habits similar to those in nineteenth-century America: a large breakfast eaten after early chores, dinner around 1 o'clock, and supper in the early evening when all chores were finished. City life is of course entirely different. In order for dinner to remain the social meal, it has been moved to evening when all the family is at home. Supper, in the Colonial sense, is now lunch.

✳ Basic Soup Stocks

It's so easy to make stocks and freeze them in small containers to have on hand for sauces, or in larger containers for quick soups. Use up those leftovers!

BEEF STOCK

1 large beef soup bone or bones, scraps, and defatted gravy from leftover roast
1 onion, chopped coarsely
2 garlic cloves
½ cup chopped parsley, or less

small piece each of green pepper, carrot and celery
1 small tomato, coarsely chopped
bay leaf
salt and pepper

Have the bones cracked with a meat cleaver or hammer so that the marrow can be fully utilized. Put all except salt and pepper in a large kettle and cover completely with water. Bring to a boil, then reduce heat to a simmer and cook for several hours, or until stock has reduced by half. Add salt and pepper and taste to adjust seasonings. Should be strong and delicious. Strain. Refrigerate stock overnight so that fat comes to the top. Skim off the fat and discard. Stock should jell if made with enough gelatin-rich bones and if reduced sufficiently. Freeze or use as desired.

CHICKEN STOCK

necks, backs, wings from fryers or hens
1 onion, coarsely chopped
1 garlic clove

¼ cup chopped parsley
a little celery and carrot
salt and pepper

Crack the bones. Place everything except salt and pepper in a large kettle; cover with water to about 1 inch over the bones. Bring to a boil, reduce heat, and simmer for several hours, or until stock has reduced by half. Add salt and pepper to taste. Strain, cool, and skim off fat.

TURKEY STOCK

all bones from leftover Thanksgiving or Christmas bird
1 onion, coarsely chopped
2 garlic cloves

¼ cup each of chopped celery and carrot
¼ cup chopped parsley
salt and pepper

Crack the bones; remove any stuffing that clings to the cavity, and discard any fatty skin. Put all ingredients except salt and pepper in a large kettle. Cover completely with water and proceed as for chicken stock. Add salt and pepper to taste when stock has finished cooking.

FISH STOCK
head, tail and bones of fish, and   *1 garlic clove*
     shrimp shells   *1 small carrot*
½ onion, chopped   *½ cup dry white wine or Vermouth*

Put all ingredients except seasoning in a large kettle, and cover with water. Simmer for about 45 minutes. Strain, and season to taste with salt and pepper.

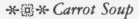

✻⚙✻ *Carrot Soup*

To 3 Pints of strong broth, a quart of carrots sliced and stewed in butter 2 oz. till they are tender. then rub them through a sieve, add a cup of full cream and stir all together—

My Mother's Cookbook
Rosa Anne Mason Grosvenor, ca. 1850

✻ Elegant Cream Soups

{ *Adapted from "Carrot Soup," Grosvenor, 1850* }

1 large yellow onion   *salt*
3 or 4 garlic cloves   *1 cup heavy cream, whipped to soft*
¼ pound butter   *peak stage and very lightly salted*
1½ pounds vegetable (carrot,   *herbs: ¼ teaspoon grated mace*
     squash, turnip, broccoli or   *with carrots; sprig of fresh*
     spinach), chopped   *marjoram with turnip; sprigs of*
2 cups strong chicken stock   *fresh mint with squash; leaf of*
1 cup half-and-half cream-and-   *fresh basil with spinach*
     milk, plus additional milk to thin
     and to taste

Chop onion and mash garlic; cook both in butter until onion is soft but not brown. Add chopped vegetables and continue cooking, tightly covered and over low heat, until vegetables are almost tender. Add stock and continue cooking for at least 30 minutes until vegetables are very soft; cool. Put through blender, a little at a time. Add half-and-half, and salt to taste. If necessary thin with milk, or add chicken broth concentrate for added interest. Heat but do not allow to boil. Garnish each serving with 1 teaspoon whipped cream and decorate with appropriate herb on top of cream. Chopped fresh parsley will do when other herbs are not available. (Put mace in carrot soup when milk is added; serve the soup with a sprig of mint on the cream.)

These soups are delicious when served cold. Put the puréed vegetable mixture in refrigerator overnight so that any excess butter will rise to the top and can be taken off easily. Add milk and cream, correct seasonings, and serve in icy bowls with whipped cream and appropriate herb. Do experiment with fresh herbs! Let your imagination and taste buds dictate your own personal touch! *Makes 8 to 10 servings.*

✳ Queens Soup

{ *Adapted from "Queens Soup,"* The Virginia Housewife, *1824* }

3 cups strong chicken stock
2 cups blanched almonds
1 bay leaf
1 tablespoon minced onion
1 teaspoon salt

1 cup heavy cream
4 egg yolks
4 tablespoons coarsely grated
   orange rind
¼ cup dry sherry

Put 1½ cups stock in blender container, add almonds, and blend until smooth. Simmer stock, almond paste, bay leaf, onion and salt for 30 minutes. Beat cream and eggs until thoroughly mixed. Cool stock mixture slightly, remove bay leaf, then add egg mixture and 3 tablespoons orange rind. Add sherry and chill for at least 3 hours. Garnish with remaining orange rind. *Makes 6 servings.*

VARIATION
Omit bay leaf, onion, sherry and orange rind and add 1/8 teaspoon almond extract and ½ cup fine-diced chicken. Garnish with minced fennel.

WOODEN ROLLING PIN

✳ Split Pea Soup (Pease Porridge)

{ *Adapted from "Dried Pea Soup," The Virginia Housewife, 1824* }

1 cup dried split peas
3½ cups strong chicken stock or
  bouillon
1 small onion, chopped

1 strip of bacon
salt and pepper
2 teaspoons olive oil
4 slices of sweet onion

Wash peas. Put them in the stock with onion, bacon, and salt and pepper to taste; simmer until peas are tender. Remove bacon. Put mixture in blender and mix until smooth. Serve hot with ½ teaspoon olive oil and a slice of sweet onion on top of each serving. Croutons are good, too. *Makes 4 servings.*

VARIATION   CREAM OF PEA SOUP
1 cup dried split peas
3½ cups strong chicken stock
1 medium-sized onion, sliced thin
1 medium-sized carrot, sliced thin

2 small lettuce leaves
1 teaspoon sugar
3 tablespoons butter
½ cup heavy cream

Wash peas. Put all ingredients except butter and cream in a pot and simmer until peas are tender, approximately 30 to 40 minutes. Place mixture in blender and mix until smooth. Place in top part of a double boiler, and stir in the butter and cream, more cream if soup is too thick. If you prefer a lighter soup use light cream. Serve hot.

✳ Sopa de Frijole

{ *A Spanish adaptation from "To Make a Harrico of French Beans," The Art of Cookery, 1796* }

1 pound dried white beans
2 tablespoons olive oil
1 tablespoon salt
1 bay leaf
5 cups strong beef stock

⅔ cup sharp Cheddar cheese
2 teaspoons green peppercorns
  (optional)
1 teaspoon minced fresh basil
dash of cayenne pepper

Wash beans well in cool water. Cover with fresh water and soak beans overnight. The next day transfer the beans and the water in which they were soaked to a kettle, and add the olive oil, salt and bay leaf. Cook until beans are done, then remove bay leaf. Measure 4 cups of the cooked beans; save any remaining for other uses. Add rest of ingredients to the measured amount of beans. Put in blender in small amounts until all is thoroughly mixed and creamy. Adjust seasonings. Reheat before serving. *Makes 8 to 10 servings.*

❋ Gazpacho

{ *Adapted from "Gaspacho-Spanish,"* The Virginia Housewife, *1824* }

2 large tomatoes, peeled
2 garlic cloves, peeled
1 large cucumber, peeled
1 medium-sized onion, peeled
1 medium-sized green pepper,
    seeded
1 small jar (4 ounces) chopped
    pimientos
1 can (24 ounces) tomato juice

⅓ cup olive oil
⅓ cup red-wine vinegar
¼ teaspoon liquid hot pepper
    seasoning
½ tablespoon salt
⅛ teaspoon black pepper
croutons
chopped chives

In a blender combine 1 tomato, 2 garlic cloves, ½ cucumber, 1 onion, ½ green pepper, pimientos with liquid, and ½ cup tomato juice. Blend at high speed for 30 seconds. Remove to a large bowl and mix with remaining tomato juice, olive oil, vinegar, hot pepper seasoning, salt and pepper; refrigerate, covered, until well chilled. Chop separately the remaining tomato, cucumber and green pepper. Place each chopped vegetable in a separate small bowl, and prepare a bowl of seasoned croutons and one of chopped chives. Serve these as accompaniments to the chilled gazpacho, served in chilled bowls. *Makes 6 to 8 servings.*

EARLY AMERICAN WIRE STRAINER

✳ Cold Grapefruit Soup

3 large or 4 small avocados
2½ cups grapefruit juice
juice of 1 lemon
1 teaspoon salt

2 teaspoons sugar
¼ teaspoon ground allspice
¼ teaspoon ground cinnamon
2 cups ice water

Mix peeled and pitted avocados in blender with 2 cups of the grapefruit juice. Add lemon juice, salt, sugar, allspice and cinnamon. Add rest of grapefruit juice and water; blend thoroughly. Serve ice cold. *Makes 8 servings.*

PAUL REVERE SILVER
TANKARD, 1795

✳ Curry Surprise

3 cans (10½ ounces each)
  condensed beef consommé with
  gelatin added
1 teaspoon unflavored gelatin
2 tablespoons water

¼ cup sherry
1 pound cream cheese
1 tablespoon curry powder
chopped parsley

Set aside half of a can of the consommé. Dissolve gelatin in the water and add sherry. Place all ingredients except for ½ can of consommé and the parsley in a blender and thoroughly blend. Pour into twelve 4-ounce ramekins or custard cups and chill in refrigerator for at least 4 hours. (Suggest preparing to this point the day before using.) Spoon 2 teaspoons plus of the reserved half-can of consommé over each dish to form a thin film. Return to refrigerator to set for approximately 3 hours. Just before serving, garnish each dish with a little minced parsley. Serve with lightly buttered brown bread. *Makes 12 servings.*

✳ Exotic Black Mushroom Soup

½ pound mushrooms (black insides
  preferred)
2 cans (10½ ounces each)
  condensed beef consommé or
  strong beef stock
2 tablespoons butter
1½ tablespoons mashed cooked
  potato

¼ cup cold water
1 tablespoon dry Vermouth
salt and pepper
4 tablespoons whipped cream, or 4
  lemon slices

Simmer mushrooms in half of the consommé or stock until tender. Remove and discard stems. Chop tops fine. Melt butter in a skillet and cook mushroom tops for 8 minutes. Add rest of consommé and simmer for 10 minutes. Add potato mixed with cold water and the Vermouth. Season to taste. Blot off any fat with paper towel. Divide into 4 ovenproof 6-ounce ramekins and put 1 heaping tablespoon of whipped cream on top of each. Slide under broiler until the cream browns on top. Serve immediately. Float 1 thin slice of lemon on top of each serving instead of whipped cream if desired. *Makes 4 servings.*

✳ Hearty Country Borscht

{ *Russian traditional* }

3 pounds stew meat, cut into 1-inch
  cubes
bacon fat
2 tablespoons salt
½ teaspoon black pepper
2 bay leaves
4 cloves
10 cups water
3 cups julienne strips of carrots
1½ cups julienne strips of onions
2 cups julienne strips of potatoes

3 cups chopped peeled tomatoes
4 cups shredded cabbage
1½ pounds knockwurst, Polish
  sausage or other good sausage,
  sliced
2 cups julienne strips of beets
⅓ cup red-wine vinegar
½ cup sugar
salt and pepper
1 cup sour cream

Brown meat in small amount of bacon fat. Add salt, pepper, bay leaves, and cloves. Cover with the water. Bring to a boil, reduce heat to low, and simmer for about 45 minutes. Remove bay leaf and cloves, and add the carrots, onions, potatoes, tomatoes and cabbage. Bring again to a boil and reduce heat. Simmer slowly for another 30 minutes. Finally, add sliced sausage, beets, vinegar and sugar. Bring to a boil once more and continue cooking for a final 30 minutes. Taste for seasoning, and add more salt and pepper if desired. Serve hot with a heaping tablespoon of sour cream on each serving. This soup does not look as attractive after the first day since beets lose their color after cooking. However, the taste is as delicious as it is the first day. Plan to make it the morning of the day it is to be served. This is a meal all by itself. *Makes 8 to 12 servings.*

❀ *Egg and Bacon Pie to eat cold.*

Steep a few thin slices of bacon all night in water to take out the salt, lay your bacon in the dish, beat eight eggs, with a pint of thick cream, put in a little pepper and salt, and pour it on the bacon, lay over it a good cold paste, bake it a day before you want it in a moderate oven.

The Art of Cookery Made Plain and Easy
Hannah Glasse, 1796

❋ **Party Quiche**

{ *Adapted from "Egg and Bacon Pie,"* The Art of Cookery, *1796* }

8 slices of bacon
1 large onion, sliced
1 tablespoon butter
1 cup heavy cream, heated
3 eggs

½ teaspoon dry mustard
10-inch pastry shell, partially cooked
1 cup grated Gruyère cheese
dash of grated nutmeg

Cook bacon until crisp, drain and crumble. Sauté onion in butter in a covered saucepan for 1 or 2 minutes, no more. Remove from heat. Add the warmed cream. Beat the eggs and mustard together and add to the cream-onion mixture. In the pastry shell, arrange the crumbled cooked bacon and cover with grated cheese. Pour the cream mixture over all.

Sprinkle with grated nutmeg and bake in 375° oven for 25 to 30 minutes. *Makes 4 to 6 servings.*

VARIATIONS

1 Substitute ham strips for the bacon.

2 Add 1 cup sautéed mushrooms to the cream mixture.

3 Add 1 cup cooked broccoli pieces, asparagus pieces, or cooked potato cubes. (The flavor of potato cubes will be improved if they are lightly sautéed in butter before adding to the quiche.)

4 Substitute ¾ cup crab meat for bacon.

5 Substitute ¾ cup cooked, chopped and well-drained spinach and a pinch of mace for the bacon.

✷ Fancy Baked Eggs

{ *Adapted from "A Fricassee of Eggs,"* The Art of Cookery, *1796* }

2 large onions, sliced
6 tablespoons butter or margarine
6 hard-cooked eggs, sliced
2 tablespoons flour
1 ⅔ cups light cream or half-and-half

1 teaspoon prepared mustard
2 tablespoons grated Swiss or Parmesan cheese
1 egg yolk, beaten

Sauté onion slices in 4 tablespoons of the butter. Layer egg slices and onion slices alternately in an 8-inch pie dish. Melt remaining butter; stir in flour. Add cream and stir over heat until thick. Add mustard and cheese. Stir beaten yolk slowly into cooled sauce. Pour the mixture over eggs and onions. Bake in 350° oven until knife comes out clean, for 25 to 30 minutes. This makes a delightful main course for lunch. Serve with salad and a nutty bread. *Makes 4 servings.*

AMERICAN WOODEN
EGG CRATE

* Scotch Eggs

{ *Adapted from "Forced Eggs," The Art of Cookery, 1796* }

12 hard-cooked eggs, shelled
1½ pounds spicy sausage meat
2 raw egg yolks
¼ cup milk

1 cup seasoned coarse fresh bread
  crumbs
cooking oil

Cover shelled eggs with a thin layer of uncooked sausage. Beat raw egg yolks and milk together thoroughly. Dip whole eggs into mixture, coating sausage layer. Then roll in bread crumbs, again being careful to coat thoroughly. Allow to stand for 30 minutes before frying. In a deep skillet, heat enough cooking oil to cover about ½ egg. Gently put eggs into hot oil and fry until golden brown on all sides. Remove and drain on paper towels. Allow to cool to room temperature. Serve with hot English mustard. *Makes 12 servings.*

The recipe below was given to Sarah Appleby Buckner by her grandmother when she began keeping house in 1830 as a bride in South Carolina. Each family in the South had its own traditional way of preparing this New Year's celebration dish. In the old tradition of Southern hospitality this makes enough to feed quite a crowd!

The contents are symbolic for good luck and happiness for the New Year: black-eyed peas and hog jowl for good luck, rice for purity, rosemary for friendship, mustard for steadfastness, bourbon for happy hours with family and friends.

* South Carolina Hoppin' John

3 pounds dried black-eyed peas
4 pounds hog jowl or breakfast
  bacon, not too lean
4 cups chopped onions
1 pound raw rice

2 teaspoons ground rosemary
2 teaspoons dry mustard
1 teaspoon hot pepper sauce
1 cup bourbon
salt

Soak peas in cold water overnight. Cut jowl or bacon into ½-inch pieces and sauté in a large iron skillet until crisp. Remove from heat and let stand at room temperature. Do not pour off grease. Add chopped onions to skillet. Cook rice until fluffy. Pour water off peas, cover them with fresh water, and cook *uncovered* over low heat until soft. (Covering the pot causes the peas to "shell out.") In a large container place rice, peas, hog jowl or bacon with grease and onions, the rosemary, mustard and hot pepper sauce. Stir *only* with a large fork so that contents remain whole and are not broken up. Place in 4 large crocks (about 2-quart size). To this point Hoppin' John may be prepared the day before serving.

Set the crocks, *uncovered*, in a pan with water that comes about halfway up sides of crocks. Allow to steam over low heat for at least 2 hours so that ingredients meld and grease is absorbed. When ready to serve, put into a very large serving container and add the bourbon. Taste for salt. Stir only with a large fork to mix well. *Makes 16 servings.*

SILVER MUSTARD SPOON,
LESCURE, PHILADELPHIA, 1830

Twentieth-century casseroles are loose adaptations of early ragoos, stews and hashes, which have been greatly improved by additional ingredients and seasonings. The following recipes have been inspired by some of those "made-dishes."

✳ Chicken or Crab Giovanni Casserole

¼ *pound butter or margarine*
2 *cups chopped onions*
1 *garlic clove, mashed*
1 *can (6 ounces) sliced mushrooms*
½ *pound vermicelli, cooked*
3 *cups 2-inch pieces of King crab meat or white meat of chicken*
½ *cup sliced stuffed olives*
½ *pound sharp Cheddar cheese, grated*

1 *cup sour cream*
1 *can (28 ounces) whole tomatoes, chopped with juice*
½ *tablespoon salt*
1 *teaspoon crushed dried basil*
⅔ *cup dry or medium sherry*
grated cheese for topping

Melt butter in a large skillet and sauté onions, garlic and mushrooms until tender. Do not brown. Combine all remaining ingredients except cheese for topping with sautéed vegetables in a large bowl and mix gently but well. Mixture will have a good amount of liquid. Pour into a well-oiled 4-

quart casserole. Let stand for 6 hours or overnight before cooking so that liquid is slowly absorbed. Top with additional grated cheese, and bake in 350° oven for 45 minutes to 1 hour. (Freezes well before final cooking.) *Makes 8 to 10 servings.*

✳ Beef-Ginger-Rice Casserole

4 tablespoons shortening or oil
1 cup matchstick pieces of cooked
    beef or pork
2 tablespoons crystallized
    gingerroot, or 2 teaspoons
    ground ginger
2 teaspoons soy sauce
¼ cup light cream

2 tablespoons water
1 bouillon cube
4 cups cooked rice, dry and fluffy
1 bunch of green onions with tops,
    chopped
8 eggs, poached

Heat shortening in a large skillet; brown meat lightly. Rinse sugar from crystallized gingerroot and chop fine; add to meat. Add rest of ingredients except green onions and eggs. Stir until mixture is thoroughly mixed and hot. Remove to a heated bowl and top generously with chopped green onions. Place poached eggs on top and serve at once. The eggs and onions will mix into rice as it is served. *Makes 8 servings.*

✳ Chicken and Green-Chili Casserole

2 large frying chickens
1 can (4 ounces) green chilies
1 medium-sized onion, chopped
2 tablespoons butter or margarine
1 can (10½ ounces) condensed
    cream of chicken soup
1 can (10½ ounces) condensed
    cream of mushroom soup

1 can (10½ ounces) condensed
    chicken stock, or homemade
    stock
12 corn tortillas
salt and pepper
½ pound Cheddar cheese, grated

Poach the frying chickens; save the cooking liquid. Bone the chickens and cut the meat into cubes. Rinse chilies, remove seeds, and chop fine. Sauté onion in butter until soft. Add chilies, undiluted soups and stock, chicken, and tortillas which have been torn into 1-inch squares. Season with salt and pepper to taste, and turn into a greased 2-quart casserole. Top with grated cheese. Bake at 350° for 35 to 45 minutes.

King Ranch Casserole is similar to this recipe, but it has one 1-pound can of tomatoes, drained and cut into pieces, added to the mixture. *Makes 8 to 10 servings.*

✳ Savory Shrimp Supper Casserole

2 pounds shelled cooked shrimps
1 tablespoon lemon juice
3 tablespoons vegetable oil
¼ cup chopped green pepper
¼ cup chopped onion
2 tablespoons butter
¾ cup rice, cooked al dente
1 teaspoon salt

¼ teaspoon pepper
dash of cayenne pepper
1 can (10½ ounces) condensed
  cream of tomato soup
½ cup sherry
½ cup slivered almonds
1 cup grated cheese
¼ teaspoon paprika

Place shrimps in a 2-quart casserole; sprinkle with lemon juice and oil. Sauté green pepper and onion in butter for about 5 minutes. Add other ingredients except ¼ cup almonds, the cheese and paprika, and pour over the shrimps. Mix cheese, paprika and remaining almonds, and sprinkle over top. Bake in 350° oven for about 50 minutes. *Makes 6 servings.*

AMERICAN EGG WHISK

✳ Bacon-Tomato Casserole

whole tomatoes, peeled and sliced
well-buttered bread slices, crusts
  removed
bacon, cooked about half-done

American cheese, shredded
chopped cooked bacon, onion and
  parsley for topping

This recipe can be varied as to proportions of ingredients according to individual taste, and can be increased or decreased according to the number of servings desired.

In a well-greased casserole or a shallow baking dish arrange a layer of sliced tomatoes. Cover with a layer of buttered bread slices, then a layer of bacon strips and, finally, shredded cheese. Repeat the layers until the dish is full. Top with a mixture of chopped bacon, onion and parsley. Bake uncovered in 350° oven until casserole is bubbly and the bread has absorbed the liquid.

NORTH CAROLINA SILVER SUGAR TONGS,
SELPH & PYLE, 1780

✳ Agnes's Gumbo

{ *Similar to "Gumbo," Grosvenor, 1850* }

1 cup plus 6 tablespoons shortening
1 cup flour
1½ pounds okra, cut into small
  pieces
1 cup onions, chopped
1 large green pepper, chopped
3 or 4 garlic cloves, minced
2 cups tomato sauce

8 cups water
½ teaspoon cayenne pepper
salt and pepper
1½ pounds shelled cooked shrimps
1 pound crab meat, picked over
  well
Gumbo filé powder (optional; see
  Note)

Melt 1 cup of shortening in a heavy skillet. Add flour and patiently stir it over medium heat until you have a rich brown roux. In another skillet melt 4 tablespoons of shortening; add okra and simmer it, covered, for 50 minutes until all slipperiness is removed. Stir it often. In a 5-quart pot melt 2 tablespoons of shortening and simmer onions and green pepper until limp. To this add garlic and tomato sauce, blend well, and then add roux. Next add okra, mix well, and then add the water. Add cayenne, and salt and pepper to taste. Bring ingredients to a boil, immediately turn heat low, cover the pot, and simmer for 40 minutes. Turn off heat and add shrimps and crab meat. Allow to sit for several hours before serving. Before heating, skim off any fat on top. Serve piping hot over hot cooked rice in large shallow soup bowls. *Makes 6 to 8 servings.*

NOTE

Gumbo filé powder is not usually added to gumbo made with okra. If you wish to add filé (powdered sassafras leaf which was originally made by the Choctaw Indians, who called it *kombo*), it must be added after gumbo has been removed from the heat. Adding it while cooking renders the gumbo stringy. Stir it in and allow gumbo to stand for 5 minutes before serving.

✳❀✳ To make an Ollo—a Spanish dish.

Take two pounds beef, one pound mutton, a chicken, or half a pullet, and a small piece of pork; put them into a pot with very little water, and set it on the fire at ten o'clock, to stew gently; you must sprinkle over it an onion chopped small, some pepper and salt, before you pour in the water; at half after twelve, put into the pot two or three apples or pears, peeled and cut in two, tomatos with the skin taken off, cimblins cut in pieces, a handful of mint chopped, lima beans, snaps, and any kind of vegetable you like; let them all stew together till three o'clock; some cellery tops cut small, and added at half after two, will improve it much.

The Virginia Housewife: or, Methodical Cook
Mrs. Mary Randolph, 1824

✳ Ollo Casserole

{ *Inspired by "To Make an Ollo—A Spanish Dish,"*
The Virginia Housewife, *1824* }

1 large onion, chopped
1 large green pepper, chopped
bacon fat
2 pounds meat, ground
3 cans (10½ ounces each)
* condensed cream of tomato soup*
1 can (20 ounces) whole-kernel
* corn*
1 jar (2 ounces) stuffed olives,
* sliced*

1 can (4½ ounces) sliced
* mushrooms*
1 pound American cheese, grated
9 ounces noodles
2 cups sliced blanched almonds
salt and pepper
Worcestershire sauce

Sauté onion and green pepper in bacon fat until tender. Add meat and brown, stirring to break meat into small pieces. Drain excess fat. Remove from heat and add soup, drained corn, sliced olives, drained mushrooms and cheese, saving some cheese to sprinkle on top. Cook noodles, drain, and add with almonds and seasonings to taste. Mix all ingredients well

96

and place in a greased flat cooking pan, or several pans; sprinkle with remaining cheese. Bake in a hot-water bath in 350° oven for 30 to 40 minutes. (Freezes well before final cooking.) *Makes 8 to 10 servings.*

✳ Shrimp Creole

*1 medium-sized onion, chopped
fine*
1 green pepper, chopped fine
*2 celery ribs with leaves, chopped
fine*
1 garlic clove, minced
4 parsley sprigs, chopped fine
¼ pound butter or margarine
6 ounces tomato paste
1 bouillon cube
½ teaspoon dried marjoram

½ teaspoon dried orégano
3 bay leaves
½ teaspoon ground allspice
½ teaspoon chili powder
1 cup water
2 cups canned tomatoes
2 teaspoons salt
1 tablespoon steak sauce
1 tablespoon Worcestershire sauce
3 pounds shelled raw shrimps

Brown onion, green pepper, celery, garlic and parsley in half of the butter. Add tomato paste, bouillon cube, herbs, spices and the water, mixing well over medium heat. Cut canned tomatoes into small pieces. Add them with remaining butter, the salt, steak and Worcestershire sauces. Simmer, uncovered, over *low* heat for about 40 minutes, or until mixture darkens and turns brown; as long as it is red it will taste too much of tomato. When mixture begins to brown, add shrimps and stir frequently while heating. Cover pan if sauce begins to stick and add another bouillon cube and 4 tablespoons butter. Serve over hot cooked rice. *Makes 6 servings.*

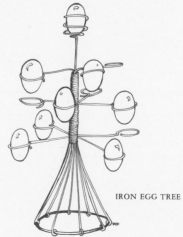

IRON EGG TREE

✻ Tortilla Rolls with Chicken
and Sour Cream

2 pounds boneless and skinless
    white meat of chicken
2 cups water
1 medium-sized onion, chopped
¼ cup chopped celery leaves
1 small bay leaf
4 parsley sprigs
salt and pepper
3 cups sour cream

2 tablespoons butter
¼ cup fine-chopped onion
1 can (4 ounces) green chilies,
    drained and chopped
8 corn tortillas
8 slices of Monterey Jack cheese
8 pitted ripe olives
8 strips of pimiento

Put chicken in a heavy saucepan with the water, next four ingredients, and salt and pepper to taste. Simmer over medium heat until chicken is just tender. Remove chicken from broth and cool. Dice chicken and reduce broth to 1 cup. Mix diced chicken, reduced broth and sour cream together, and set aside. Melt butter in a skillet, and cook chopped onion in it until tender. Add chopped chilies and the chicken mixture. Soften tortillas in an ungreased hot skillet or under water. Roll each one around 1/3 cup of the chicken mixture, and place them in a single layer in a greased casserole. Ladle the rest of the chicken mixture over the filled rolls. Put a slice of cheese, an olive and a pimiento strip on each roll. Bake at 375° for 20 minutes. *Makes 4 servings.*

✻ Chile Tostadas

bacon fat
12 flour tortillas
1 recipe Chile con Carne (p. 43)
1 pound medium-sharp cheese,
    grated
3 large tomatoes, peeled and
    chopped

¼ head lettuce, shredded
1 bunch of green onions, chopped
1 large can (10 ounces) taco sauce
1 cup sour cream (optional)

In a large heavy iron skillet, melt bacon fat to about 1½ inches in depth, and heat until smoking. Dip each tortilla into hot water and place immediately in hot fat. Take care with this, as the water makes the fat pop and spatter. Fry for about 1 minute, and turn to brown both sides. Tortilla should be slightly puffed, brown and crisp when tapped. Remove and drain on paper towel.

Arrange tortillas on a large jellyroll pan or individual ovenproof plates. Allow two per person. On each tortilla, spoon 6 to 8 tablespoons of chile con carne, as much as each will hold. Sprinkle 2 to 3 tablespoons grated cheese on top and run under broiler until cheese is melted. Garnish each tortilla with generous amounts of chopped tomato, lettuce and green onion. Serve immediately, with taco sauce. Add 1 tablespoon sour cream to each one if desired. *Makes 6 servings.*

✳ Oyster and Turkey Casserole

{ *Adapted from "To Stew Oysters,"* The Art of Cookery, *1796* }

6 ounces butter
¾ cup flour
6 ounces deviled ham
¼ teaspoon pepper
6 cups milk or stock
½ cup cornstarch

3 cups diced leftover turkey (more
   if desired)
2 pints oysters, with liquor
good dash of grated nutmeg
salt
chopped parsley

Melt butter and add flour, stirring to make a light roux. Add deviled ham and pepper, and stir in milk or stock that has been mixed with cornstarch. Cook until thick, stirring constantly. Add turkey, drained oysters and seasonings to taste. Thin with oyster liquor if needed, or thicken with a little more cornstarch. Serve over hot fluffy rice, sprinkled with chopped parsley. *Makes 10 servings.*

✳ Beef and Cabbage Casserole

{ *Inspired by "Bubble and Squeak"* }

1 pound ground beef
1 cup chopped onions
1 cup uncooked rice
2 cups canned tomatoes
½ tablespoon cuminseeds, crushed

salt and pepper
4 cups beef stock or bouillon
1 medium-size head of cabbage,
   chopped

Sauté meat in a hot skillet until brown; remove. Sauté onions and rice in same skillet until brown. Drain excess fat and return meat to pan with rice and onions. Add tomatoes, cuminseeds, and seasonings to taste, and cook for about 12 minutes. Pour 2 cups of stock into the mixture and continue cooking until rice is tender. In a greased 3-quart casserole place alternate layers of chopped cabbage and the meat mixture, ending with the meat on top. Pour the remaining 2 cups of stock over the cabbage and meat mixture and cover. Bake at 400° for about 1 hour. *Makes 6 servings.*

VARIATION
Omit cuminseeds and substitute 1 teaspoon dried basil, 1 teaspoon orégano, and 1 garlic clove chopped fine.

✳ Cleto's Game-Bird Pie

{ *Variation of "Another Method of Making a Chicken Pie,"* The Housekeeper's Instructor, *1798* }

1 recipe Basic Pastry (p. 72)
16 birds (8 quails, 8 doves)
2 tablespoons olive oil
1 large onion, chopped
1 teaspoon salt
¾ teaspoon black pepper
½ teaspoon garlic salt
1 tablespoon ground cuminseed
¼ teaspoon dried thyme

2 tablespoons flour
1 canned jalapeño pepper without
 seeds
1 teaspoon Worcestershire sauce
1 cup bite-size pieces of carrot
1 cup green peas
1 cup green beans
1 cup bite-size pieces of celery

Make the pastry first. Roll it into a round large enough to cover the baking dish. Roll up the round in wax paper and keep in a cool place, or in the refrigerator, until needed. Remove breasts of birds. Remove skin. Cut breasts into bite-sized pieces. Save legs to deep-fry for a later meal. Simmer the bones, except for the legs, to make a stock; reduce to 3 cups and strain.

Pour the olive oil into a large heavy skillet with heatproof handle. Sauté bird pieces and onion until they are light brown, 10 to 15 minutes. Add salt, black pepper, garlic salt, cuminseed, thyme, flour (stir in rapidly), jalapeño pepper, Worcestershire and the strained bird stock. Stir thoroughly, cover skillet, and put into a 300° oven for 1 to 1½ hours.

In boiling salted water, cook carrots, peas, green beans and celery separately for 15 minutes. Drain vegetables. After birds have cooked, remove skillet from oven and stir in the drained vegetables. Put whole mixture in large round baking dish, about 3-quart size. Place the pastry round over the top; put a few fork holes in it for steam. Bake at 375° for 25 to 30 minutes, until crust is golden brown. *Makes 8 servings.*

✻⊛✻ *Salmagundy for a Middle-Dish at Supper.*

In the top plate in the middle, which should stand higher than the rest, take a fine pickled-herring, bone it, take off the head and mince the rest fine; in the other plates round put the following things: in one pare a cucumber and cut it very thin; in another, apples pared and cut small; in another, an onion peeled and cut small; in another, two hard eggs chopped small, the whites in one and the yolks in another; pickled girkins cut small; in another celery cut small; in another pickled red cabbage chopped fine; take some water-cresses clean washed and picked, stick them all about and between every plate or saucer, and throw nastertium-flowers about the cresses. You must have oil and vinegar, and lemon, to eat with it. If it is neatly set out, it will make a pretty figure in the middle of the table, or you may lay them in heaps in a dish: if you have not all these ingredients set out your plates or saucers with just what you fancy, and in the room of a pickled-herring you may mince anchovies.

The Art of Cookery Made Plain and Easy
Hannah Glasse, 1796

✻ Salmagundy

{ *Adapted from "Salmagundy for a Middle-Dish at Supper,"* The Art of Cookery, *1796* }

Arrange dishes of cold cooked vegetables such as broccoli, cauliflower, asparagus, kidney beans, etc., which have been marinated in French dressing; other dishes of sliced sweet onions, sliced cucumbers, halved cherry tomatoes, thin-sliced celery, sliced radishes, chopped hard-cooked eggs, anchovies, croutons, Parmesan cheese, and a large bowl of lettuces. Have several types of dressing. Let your guests "build" their own salads. Serve with cold sliced meats, herring, smoked salmon, lobster tails or crab claws. Add watermelon pickles, spiced peaches and crab apples for garnish. To dress the seafood, serve homemade mayonnaise or a dressing made of equal parts of sour cream and avocado, salted to taste and seasoned with cuminseed.

* Greek Grape Salad

{ *Variation on "Salmagundy,"* The Art of Cookery, *1796* }

1 red onion, sliced thin
1 teaspoon sugar
1 cup halved Thompson seedless grapes
1 cup halved and seeded Tokay grapes

2 oranges, sections only
1 cup crumbled Feta cheese
1 bunch of watercress
4 tablespoons olive oil
lemon juice
salt and white pepper

Slice onion and let stand in a bowl of ice water to which the sugar has been added for about 15 minutes. Drain well and add next six ingredients, tossing to mix well. Add lemon juice to taste, and season with salt and white pepper. *Makes 4 servings.*

* Eggplant Salad

3 medium-sized eggplants, about 3 pounds
2 tablespoons lemon juice
1 tablespoon plus 1 teaspoon salt
2 tablespoons cider vinegar
2 tablespoons dry vermouth
6 tablespoons olive oil
1 teaspoon garlic powder

¼ cup chopped parsley
¾ cup fine-chopped celery
⅓ cup fine-chopped green onions, including tops
½ cup thin green-pepper strips
12 thick slices of large tomatoes
½ cup sour cream

Peel and cube eggplants. Cook in water to which lemon juice and 1 tablespoon salt have been added. Cook until barely tender, 5 to 10 minutes.

Drain immediately. Make a dressing of vinegar, vermouth, remaining salt, olive oil and garlic powder, and pour over hot eggplant. Let cool completely at room temperature. Add parsley, and refrigerate for at least 6 hours. Add celery, green onions and green-pepper strips, and mix thoroughly but gently. Serve icy cold over the tomato slices, and garnish with sour cream, about 1 tablespoon per serving. *Makes 6 servings.*

✻ Bacon, Cucumber and Sour-Cream Salad

8 *slices of bacon, cut into ½-inch*
    pieces
4 *green onions, chopped*
2 *medium-sized cucumbers, sliced*
    thin
½ *tablespoon salt*

½ *cup sour cream*
1 *tablespoon vinegar*
1 *tablespoon sugar*
½ *teaspoon pepper*
lettuce leaves

Cook bacon in a heavy skillet. When crisp, remove and drain on absorbent paper. Put green onions and cucumbers in a bowl and stir in salt. Let stand for 30 minutes, then press as much water as possible out of cucumber. Drain well and stir in sour cream, vinegar and seasonings. Serve on lettuce leaves. *Makes 4 servings.*

✻✻✻ *French Sallad*

Chop three anchovies, a shalot and some parseley small; put them in a bowl with two tablespoonfulls of vinegar, one of oil, a little mustard, and salt. When well mixed, add by degrees some cold roast or boiled meat in the very thinnest slices; put in a few at a time, they being small, not exceeding two or three inches long; shake them in the seasoning, and then put more; cover the bowl close; and let the sallad be prepared three hours before it be eaten. Garnish with parseley, and a few slices of the fat.

A New System of Domestic Cookery, 1807

✳ Roast-Beef Salad

{ Adapted from "French Sallad," A New System of Domestic Cookery, 1807 }

ANCHOVY DRESSING

⅔ cup olive oil
1 can (2 ounces) flat anchovies, drained
3 tablespoons vinegar
3 tablespoons lemon juice

1 small garlic clove
½ teaspoon dry mustard
¼ teaspoon each of onion salt, celery salt, paprika and sugar

Blend all ingredients in a blender until smooth. *Makes enough dressing for 6 to 8 salads.*

ROAST-BEEF SALAD

Slice leftover roast beef into thin strips and marinate in anchovy dressing for several hours. Serve in a bowl of lettuces (several varieties) torn into pieces, topped with red onion rings and quartered hard-cooked eggs.

EARLY WORCESTER
SWEETMEAT DISH

✳ Lobster Salad

{ Adapted from "Lobster Salad," The Practical Housewife, 1860 }

yolks of 2 hard-cooked eggs, mashed
2 teaspoons Dijon mustard
1 tablespoon vinegar
2 tablespoons olive oil
2 tablespoons cream
1 or 2 anchovies (optional), mashed

salt and pepper
½ cup thin-sliced celery
1 cup thin-sliced cucumber
½ cup pickled beets, sliced thin
2 green onions, tops included, chopped
2½ to 3 cups lobster pieces
lettuce

Mix the well-mashed egg yolks with mustard, vinegar, oil, cream and mashed anchovies. Do not add salt or pepper until you have tasted. Mix celery, cucumber, beets and onions well with the dressing. Gently fold in seafood pieces. Serve in a bowl of lettuces or mixed with several cups of torn lettuce pieces. *Makes 4 to 6 servings.*

VARIATION
Instead of lobster, you can make this with shrimps or lump crab meat.

✳ Neptune's Cold Lunch

{ *Variation on "Lobster Salad,"* The Practical Housewife, *1860* }

4 green onions with tops, chopped
   fine
3 *green apples, peeled and chopped*
¼ *cup vegetable oil*
2 *to 3 teaspoons curry powder*
2 *teaspoons celery seeds*
2 *teaspoons dry mustard*
⅓ *cup sour cream*

1½ *cups mayonnaise*
juice of 1 lemon
¼ *cup chopped parsley*
2 *cups cooked rice*
¾ *pound lobster, King crab, or*
   lump crab meat
1 *pound cooked cleaned shrimps*
salt and white pepper

Sauté green onions and apples in oil until just soft; do not brown. Add curry powder, celery seeds and mustard; cool. Stir in sour cream, mayonnaise, lemon juice and half of parsley. Gently combine cooked rice, seafood and dressing, adjusting salt and pepper to taste. Place in a serving dish and sprinkle rest of parsley on top. Refrigerate for several hours before serving to allow flavors to meld. *Makes 6 to 8 servings.*

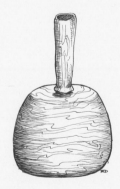

WOODEN SAUERKRAUT PRESS

✻ Hot Chicken Salad

2 tablespoons grated onion
2 tablespoons fresh lemon juice
½ teaspoon salt
1 cup mayonnaise
2 cups diced chicken (see Note)

2 cups diced celery
½ cup chopped toasted almonds
1 cup grated sharp cheese
1 cup crushed potato chips

Mix onion, lemon juice and salt with mayonnaise. Fold into chicken and let chicken marinate overnight. Next day add diced celery, stirring gently. Pour into a greased 2-quart casserole from which chicken will be served. Sprinkle almonds over the top, then grated cheese, finally the crushed potato chips. Cook in 450° oven for about 10 minutes, until chicken is heated through and cheese melted. Serve at once.

Button mushrooms and sliced water chestnuts may be added for variation. Thin slices of ham and hot curried fruits are ideal accompaniments to this dish. *Makes 6 servings.*

NOTE
While leftover baked hens were used traditionally, fryers, freshly cooked, are as delicious.

✻ Great-Grandmother's Chicken Salad

6 cups small pieces of cooked
  chicken
2½ cups fine-chopped celery
½ cup chopped sour pickles, or
  more

1 cup fine-shredded cabbage
salt and pepper

COOKED DRESSING
1 teaspoon dry mustard
1 teaspoon sugar
2 teaspoons salt

½ cup plus 2 tablespoons apple-
  cider vinegar
4 eggs

Make this the day before. First mix chicken, celery, pickles and cabbage. Then make the dressing. Mix mustard, sugar and salt. Add vinegar, stirring constantly. Beat eggs well and pour vinegar mixture slowly into them, beating all the time. Place over low heat and continue stirring until dressing thickens; do not overcook or it will curdle. When slightly cool, mix into chicken-cabbage-celery-pickle mixture. If more moisture is needed, add a little chicken stock. Taste to correct seasonings; this salad should be tangy. It must stand overnight in the refrigerator before serving. *Makes 6 to 8 servings.*

✳ Greengage Plum Salad

2 cans (16 ounces each) greengage
    plums
1 package (3 ounces) lemon-
    flavored gelatin
1 cup hot water
3 ounces cream cheese, cubed

1 avocado, cubed
½ cup pecan pieces, or ½ cup fine-
    chopped celery
12 large lettuce leaves
sour cream for topping
poppy seeds

Drain the plums, saving the syrup, and cut plums into small pieces. Heat 1 cup syrup from plums and pour over gelatin with 1 cup hot water. Allow gelatin to cool until slightly thickened. Fold in cream cheese, avocado, pecans or celery, and plum pieces. Turn into an oiled 6-cup mold or 12 individual ½-cup molds. Refrigerate for several hours to set. Unmold on a lettuce leaf; garnish with a small amount of sour cream and sprinkle poppy seeds on top. *Makes 12 servings.*

✳ Grape-Juice and Apple Salad

1 cup boiling water
1 package (3 ounces) lemon-
    flavored gelatin
½ cup grape juice
2 tablespoons lemon juice
¼ teaspoon salt
1 cup fine-chopped celery
1 cup chopped, unpeeled tart apples

½ cup raisins
½ cup chopped Cheddar cheese
lettuce leaves
⅔ cup sour cream
⅓ cup mayonnaise
1 teaspoon curry powder, or more
salt

Pour boiling water over gelatin and stir until gelatin dissolves. Add grape juice, lemon juice and salt. Chill until slightly thick. Add celery, apples, raisins and cheese. Pour into an oiled 6-cup mold. Let chill for 3 to 4 hours, or until set. Unmold on a bed of lettuce. Make a dressing with sour cream and mayonnaise, seasoned with curry powder and salt to taste. Serve dressing separately, or divide among individual servings. *Makes 6 servings.*

✳ Egg Salad Ring

2 envelopes unflavored gelatin
½ cup cold water
1 cup boiling water
¼ cup lemon juice
½ teaspoon salt
½ cup minced parsley

½ cup minced onion
¼ cup minced green pepper
2 cups mayonnaise
12 hard-cooked eggs, minced
salad greens
2 pints cherry tomatoes

Soften gelatin in cold water. Add boiling water and stir until gelatin is dissolved. Stir in lemon juice, salt, parsley, onion, green pepper and mayonnaise. Add eggs and mix thoroughly. Pour into a buttered 2-quart mold, and chill until firm. Unmold on a bed of greens. Fill center with cherry tomatoes, sliced into halves. *Makes 8 to 10 servings.*

WILLIAM WILLS
PEWTER TEA POT

✳ French Dressing

{ *Variation of "Tarragon Vinegar," Miss Leslie's*
Directions for Cookery, *1839* }

½ cup red-wine vinegar, or ¼ cup
cider vinegar mixed with ¼ cup
dry wine
1 garlic clove, mashed

1 teaspoon salt
2 tablespoons prepared Dijon
mustard
1 cup good olive oil

Mix vinegar, garlic, salt and mustard until salt is thoroughly dissolved. Add olive oil and shake well. Delicious on almost all green salads and cold vegetables. *Makes 1½ cups.*

NOTE
French olive oil is light and delicate, Sicilian the strongest flavored. Various Italian and Spanish olive oils range in between. The one you choose is a matter of taste, but be sure to buy a good fresh oil.

❋ Cooked Cream Salad Dressing
(for cold chicken salad)

3 egg yolks
½ teaspoon salt
dash of cayenne pepper
1 teaspoon dry mustard

4 tablespoons vinegar
½ teaspoon sugar
4 tablespoons butter, melted
¾ cup whipped cream

Beat egg yolks well. Add seasonings and mustard, and mix well. Stir in vinegar and sugar; lastly, add melted butter. Place in top part of a double boiler and stir constantly over steaming water until dressing thickens. Do not overcook. When cold, fold in the whipped cream. *Makes about 2 cups.*

❋ Sauterne-Poached Pears with Cream

{ *Adapted from "Baked Pears,"* Grosvenor, 1850 }

6 whole pears
1½ cups sauterne
1 cup light brown sugar, or more
12 to 18 thin strips of lemon peel
1 teaspoon lemon juice

3 tablespoons butter
½ cup light rum, warmed
1 cup whipped cream, or more,
    slightly sweetened and flavored
    with vanilla extract

Peel, halve, and core the pears (any kind; a good way to use hard cooking pears). Put pears, wine, sugar, lemon peel and juice, and butter in a shallow enamelware pan. (Add a little more brown sugar if pears are not very sweet.) Cover pan and poach pears over low heat until tender; time varies according to variety of pear. When pears are tender, remove them to a chafing dish. Cook liquid until syrupy, then pour over pears. To this point can be done early in the day.

At serving time heat pears in syrup in the chafing dish. Have ready the warmed rum. Pour rum over fruit and ignite. When flames die out, serve pears with cold whipped cream, not whipped too stiff. *Makes 6 servings.*

VARIATION
An alternate sauce, delicious on fruits, gingerbread, strawberries, etc., can be made with 1 pound cream cheese, creamed with ¾ cup dark brown sugar and a little grated lemon rind. Make early in the day so sugar dissolves completely.

EARLY WORCESTER SWEETMEAT
BASKET WITH RELISH DISHES

❋ Stuffed Pears in Rum

{ *Adapted from "Baked Pears,"* Grosvenor, *1850* }

½ *cup apricot jam*
¼ *cup sugar*
⅓ *cup water*
2 tablespoons grated lemon rind

6 pears, peeled, halved, and cored
¾ *cup chopped mixed candied*
fruits
¼ *cup rum*

In a flat pan combine jam, sugar, water and lemon rind. Add pears, cover, and poach until tender. Soak chopped candied fruits in rum for several hours. Fill each pear half with 1 tablespoon of the candied-fruit mixture. Arrange pears on a serving dish. Cook apricot sauce down until quite thick, and spoon some over each pear. Serve hot. *Makes 6 servings.*

VARIATION
Peaches or nectarines can be prepared in the same way.

❋ Bananas in Rum

{ *Variation on "Baked Pears,"* Grosvenor, *1850* }

6 tablespoons butter
9 tablespoons dark brown sugar
6 whole bananas

½ *cup light or dark rum, warmed*
ice cream mixed with rum

In a chafing dish melt butter and brown sugar. Cook peeled bananas in the mixture, with cover on dish, until bananas are fairly soft, turning once to cover them completely with juices. Have the warmed rum ready. Pour rum over bananas and ignite. When flames die out, serve with a sauce made of good vanilla ice cream softened and mixed with a little rum. *Makes 6 servings.*

✳ Fresh Grape Crunch

4 pounds green Thompson seedless
grapes, washed and stemmed

2 pints sour cream
1 pound dark brown sugar

In a deep pie dish or other suitable ovenproof 3-quart container, combine the grapes and sour cream, and put into refrigerator. About 1 hour before serving time, cover the top of this mixture with a layer of brown sugar and run it under the broiler to melt. Repeat this process until the sugar is used up and there is a good, crisp sugar crust over the top. Serve at the table in your best crystal bowls or dessert plates. This dessert is really as good the second day, served cold. *Makes 8 to 10 servings.*

✳ Fruits in Wine

(to serve with Cheese)

{ *Variation of "To preserve Peaches,"* The Art of Cookery, *1796* }

Dried fruits which have been marinated in wine for about 1 week are a delicious accompaniment to cheese for dessert. Try any of these:

pitted prunes in Madeira
apricots in sherry
raisons in Cognac (also great with roast beef)
dates in dry sherry
figs in Port or sweet sherry

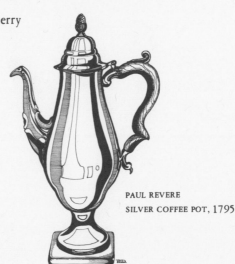

PAUL REVERE
SILVER COFFEE POT, 1795

111

✳ Hot Curried Fruits

1 can (16 ounces) peach halves
1 can (16 ounces) pear halves
1 can (16 ounces) apricot halves
1 jar (8 ounces) maraschino
  cherries (optional)

⅜ pound butter, melted
1 cup brown sugar
2 teaspoons curry powder

Drain fruits well, overnight if possible. Arrange in a shallow glass casserole and pour over them a mixture of butter, brown sugar and curry powder. Cover and bake in 300° oven for about 1 hour. If desired, a little finely chopped crystallized gingerroot can be sprinkled over the fruits before baking. This makes a fine accompaniment to Hot Chicken Salad (see Index) for a brunch. *Makes 8 servings.*

PAINTED HANGING
SPICE CABINET, 1820

Drinking

"Mind your P's and Q's," called out the tavern keeper at closing time, and the obliging men threw back their heads to get the last drop of ale from their tankards. Then into the night tumbled the boisterous Colonials, their tongues and bodies loosened from an evening of heavy drinking. This expression was later used by mothers to scold their children and make them mindful of their manners; but to the early tavern keeper it meant "Drink up! And let us all be off to bed!" Because those elegant old pewter tankards had to be poured into molds, they came in only two sizes, pints and quarts, thus giving rise to the expression "Mind your P's and Q's."

The lower- and middle-class settlers brought with them from the old world the extremely popular custom of tavern drinking. But let us not be too harsh on those lusty men downing their bumpers, or condemn them for their excessive drinking habits. First, understand some of the circumstances they all shared. There was no escaping the harsh wilderness, no retreat to warmth and safety. Second, we joke today about alcoholic beverages having medicinal value but it was no joke then, in a life that afforded no means of sanitary treatment. For example, liquor was considered good protection against the dread malaria. Third, the courageous pioneers faced tragedy almost daily. Death was a constant companion as the result of accidents, epidemics, hunger and cold. The English loved their beer and ale, the French their wines, and the Germans their schnapps, and strong spirits helped those early settlers face the hardships of pioneer life.

Of course, not all drinking was alcoholic in Colonial America. Lemonade was a special treat and very fashionable, as was ginger beer. "Bevrige" was the forerunner of our soft drinks and was made from spring water, molasses and ginger. Sailors called it "switchel" and added vinegar and rum. Tea has already been discussed. Coffee and hot chocolate were the other favorite nonalcoholic drinks during the early years in America. These were not plentiful until the eighteenth century. Coffee and chocolate beans were blended by only a few merchants in the cities and so were not widely available or affordable.

The following quote is from an early Texas traveler who recorded, "The Texas hunter buys his coffee raw and roasts it over his campfire until it is perfectly black and every particle of agreeable aroma and flavour has been dissipated, then he puts it in a shot sack and pounds it on the wagon wheel with the heel of his boot until it is sufficiently reduced. Of this charcoal-like powder he puts perhaps a half-pint into a quart of water and boils from fifteen to thirty minutes, supplying the loss by evaporation with more liquid. This he drinks without milk or sugar. Such a decoction has a taste that one might expect from a broth made of burnt hair and feathers. But the Texan likes it; he calls it coffee, drinks it for coffee, and satisfies himself that he has really drunk a cup of that delicious beverage."

There are conflicting stories as to whether or not children drank. There is much evidence of their having cider and beer in the seventeenth century. When we realize what a short time they were allowed to remain children, we can readily understand their being treated as men and women by ten years of age. As time went on and city life developed there is less evidence of children drinking. One Philadelphia little girl was shocked when offered a glass of wine for dinner. Some years earlier, however, in Boston, 1719, an eight-year-old girl from Barbados complained by letter to her fa-

EARLY AMERICAN PEWTER TANKARD

ENGLISH DELFT POSSET POT

ther that her Boston housemistress gave her water. Her father, furious, insisted she be given beer or wine, befitting her station. Children sometimes courteously toasted their parents with wine before meals. They did not indulge in "strong waters," such as gin and brandy. The trend was certainly for children to drink less as the country grew and they were allowed to enjoy childhood for a longer period of time.

Any time was a good time for drinking in the Colonies! Upon rising the downing of a mug of cider was considered customary. Apprentices and journeymen received grog from their masters as "coffee breaks" during the day. Freemen farm workers had a "pull at the jug" every other round of the field. Excuses were not necessary for drinking, as hardly an hour passed that did not provide reason enough to imbibe, be it mealtime, feast, celebration, or just plain thirst. At meals during the seventeenth century, a bowl of cider, beer or "noggin" was passed after the host had first toasted his guests with a swallow.

The daily habits of Dr. Alexander Hamilton during his 1744 trip give us a hint of what drinking was like among the gentry. His days began quite early as he would ride forth from his night's lodging around 5 o'clock, usually because he had not been pleased with his surroundings or company. He would breakfast around 9 o'clock when he came upon another tavern. He rode on until dinnertime, which often coincided with his stopping place for the next night. In the cities he remained several days. There he enjoyed the company of the ladies at tea, after which he visited a coffeehouse for an hour of backgammon. At 7 P.M. he took himself off to the most prominent tavern in the community, where would be found one of the men's clubs or philosophical societies. These met in private rooms in the taverns. Dr. Hamilton had entrées to all the best ones, or so he said. In these clubrooms, amid much drinking, serious discussions were held on politics, medicine, philosophy and gossip. Tavern food did not merit mention by Dr. Hamilton but he did mention the Madeiras, Ports and other wines, and often the company. In Philadelphia, he recalls, "I dined at a tavern with a very mixed company . . . Scots, English, Dutch, Germans, and Irish; there were Roman Catholicks, Church-

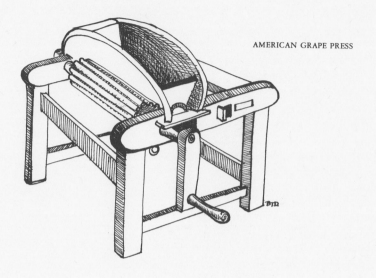

AMERICAN GRAPE PRESS

men, Presbyterians, Quakers, Newlightmen, Methodists, Seventhdaymen, Moravians, Anabaptists, and one Jew. The whole company consisted of twenty-five, planted round an oblong table; in a great hall well stocked with flies."

"The company divided into committees in conversation, the prevailing topick was politicks and conjectures of a French war." At a New York private club he warns, "To drink stoutly with the Hungarian Club, who are all bumper men, is the readiest way for a stranger to recommend himself, and a set among them are very fond of making a stranger drunk. To talk bawdy and to have a knock at punning passes among some there for good sterling wit." To cast and scour (vomit) was an expected and accepted accomplishment and a fitting conclusion to such an evening.

The scene in the common room of the taverns presents quite a different picture. There, all was chaos! As each guest arrived, it was the custom that everyone assembled make him a toast. Many other toasts were going on simultaneously. As the room filled, confusion reigned. Tankards and "firing glasses" were banged on the table after each toast and, to add to the din, entertainers often arrived playing violins or flutes, or singing. Dr. Hamilton noted, "Two or three toapers in the company seemed to be of opinion that a man could not have a more sociable quality or enduement than to be able to pour down seas of liquor and remain unconquered while others sank under the table."

There were many popular mixed drinks that were served most often at special occasions. Some of these were "caudle," a hot custardy drink with wine; "possett," milk, ale, spices and bread crumbs; "metheglin," honey, herbs and wine; hot toddies, numerous punches, and "blackstrap," which was made from molasses and rum. Mint juleps, old-fashioneds and other mixed hard-liquor drinks became known as time went by and the cocktail hour was introduced.

Political office seekers did not miss the chance to entice votes with campaign whiskey bottles. The man running for election would have bottles made up bearing his name and picture, fill them with whiskey, and hand them out to potential voters. Lavish tables were set out at the polling booths by office seekers. Many men had to travel great distances to cast their votes, and the prize at the end spurred them on. In the Virginia election of 1758, candidate George Washington's bill included charges for 146½ gallons of rum, punch, beer, wine and brandy for a few hundred voters. Needless to say, he won!

There was just as much drinking in the homes as in the public places. While whiskey was not considered "proper spirits" for gentlemen of the eighteenth century, decanters of brandy, Madeira, or sherry stood on the side tables. When gentlemen callers arrived, a bowl of loaf sugar and a pitcher of water (hot, if in winter) were brought forth so the visitor could prepare himself a drink. It would have been considered rude not to offer such refreshment. The country folk, less sophisticated, might not follow this example but it is safe to say grog or cider was available for visitors.

One cannot help but wonder what the early settlers of this country would think of the smoke-filled rooms, jammed with men and women unable to hear each other's shouting attempts at inane conversation as they "enjoy" the twentieth-century cocktail party. Were it not for the presence of women, they might liken it to the bawdy common room of a Colonial tavern.

✳❀✳ To Make a Shrub

Take two quarts of brandy, and put it in a large bottle, adding to it the juice of five lemons, the peels of two, and half a nutmeg. Stop it up, let it stand three days, and add to it three pints of white wine, and a pound and a half of sugar. Mix it, strain it twice through a flannel, and bottle it up. It is a pretty wine and a cordial.

The New England Cookery
Lucy Emerson, 1808

✳ Shrub

{ *Adapted from "To Make a Shrub,"* The New England Cookery, *1808* }

4 quarts brandy	*2½ nutmegs, cracked*
juice of 5 lemons	*3 bottles of dry white wine*
strips of peel from 2 lemons	*1 pound sugar*

Into a large crock or bottle pour brandy, lemon juice and peel, and nutmegs. Cover with cloth or paper and let stand in a cool dark place for 10 days. Add the wine and sugar, and stir until sugar is dissolved. Let stand for 3 weeks. Strain well and serve in decanters. Keeps indefinitely. Makes an unusual after-dinner drink, and 1 to 2 tablespoons is good in a cup of hot tea on a cold afternoon. *Makes about 7 quarts.*

✳ Rum Punch

8 heaping teaspoons green tea leaves	*juice of 4 lemons; save peels*
1 quart boiling water	*½ cup sugar*
	1 quart light rum

Put tea in boiling water and steep until dark. Mix lemon juice and sugar and set aside. Place lemon peels in tea and allow the tea to cool. Strain tea into lemon-sugar mixture. Add rum. Bottle and store in refrigerator.*Makes about 2 quarts.*

SUGGESTION
Serve in a punch bowl over a cake of ice. Float 1 or 2 gardenias in the punch for a "Rebel" touch.

✳ Apple Toddy

{ *Adapted from Mrs. Janvier's diary* }

1½ ounces brandy	*1 cinnamon stick, or dash of*
⅔ cup hot apple juice, approximately	*ground cinnamon*

Pour brandy into a mug and fill with hot apple juice. Put the cinnamon stick in the mug, or sprinkle ground cinnamon on top. Serve hot. *Makes 1 serving.*

✳ Wassail

{ *Adapted from "Mrs. Bush's Good Mulled Wine,"* Grosvenor, *1850* }

⅓ *cup water*
2 teaspoons ground cinnamon
1 teaspoon ground ginger
1 teaspoon ground allspice
½ *teaspoon grated nutmeg*

¼ *teaspoon ground cloves*
4 cups sugar
4 quarts claret
14 eggs, separated

Heat water and spices. Boil for about 1 minute. Add sugar and stir until sugar is dissolved. Add claret and heat but do not boil. Beat egg whites stiff. Beat yolks until thick and lemony. Fold whites into yolks. Put egg mixture in punch bowl and pour hot spiced wine into it. Whip with a wire whisk till frothy.

For a festive touch, float heated, drained, spiced crab apples in the punch bowl. *Makes 20 servings.*

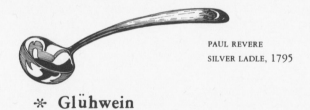

PAUL REVERE
SILVER LADLE, 1795

✳ Glühwein

{ *Traditional German* }

4 quarts Burgundy wine
juice of 1 lemon
juice of 1 orange
2 cups sugar
15 cloves

5 cinnamon sticks
1 teaspoon grated nutmeg
2 cups water
½ *cup brandy or rum*

Mix all ingredients together in a large kettle, and heat but do not boil. Serve in mugs, with a thin slice of orange and a stick of cinnamon in each mug. *Makes about 5 quarts.*

✴ Syllabub

{ Adapted from "To Make a Whipped Syllabub," The Frugal Housewife, 1772 }

3 tablespoons sugar
1 cup heavy cream
1 teaspoon grated lemon rind

1 teaspoon lemon juice
½ cup wine
2 egg whites, beaten to soft peaks

Blend sugar into cream with a wire whisk. Add lemon rind and juice and wine, and blend well. Fold in beaten egg whites and continue to hand-beat with whisk till thoroughly blended, about 5 minutes. *Makes 6 servings.*

EARLY SHEFFIELD SNUFF BOX, 1778

✴ Hot Spicy Children's Punch

4 cinnamon sticks
12 whole cloves
¼ cup packed brown sugar
2 cups water

1 can (46 ounces) pineapple juice
1 bottle (16 ounces) cranberry-juice
cocktail

Simmer spices, brown sugar and water for 10 minutes. Remove from heat, cover, and cool. Strain and discard spices. Combine spiced syrup with pineapple juice and cranberry-juice cocktail. Heat to simmering. *Makes about 2½ quarts.*

✴ Bayou Benders

{ Miss Ima Hogg's "old-fashion" family recipe }

1 tablespoon honey
1 orange, sliced thin

1 bottle (⅘ quart) good Kentucky
bourbon (not sour mash)

Place honey and orange in top part of a double boiler and steep over steaming water until orange peel is soft, about 1½ hours. Add water to the lower pan as needed to keep the water steaming at a steady rate. Pour into a jar and add bourbon. Let stand for 30 hours. Strain and bottle. Keeps indefinitely.

To serve, pour 2 jiggers over ice with a dash each of Angostura and orange bitters. Garnish with a slice of orange and a cherry. One mint sprig adds to the taste and color.

✳ Mrs. Fowler's Curaçao*

*2 quarts brandy
rind of 4 oranges, cut into 6 or 8
   pieces
rind of 4 lemons, cut into 6 or 8
   pieces*

*1½ pounds sugar
pinch of saffron*

Pour the spirit onto the other ingredients and let the whole stand for 4 days, stirring frequently. Strain and bottle. It should be quite clear and oily. *Makes about 2 quarts.*

✳❁✳ *To pot Cheshire Cheese.*

Take three pounds of Cheshire cheese, and put it into a mortar with half a pound of the best fresh butter you can get, pound them together, and in the beating add a gill of rich Canary wine, and half an ounce of mace finely beat, then sifted like fine powder; when all is extremely well mixed, press it hard down into a gallipot, cover it with clarified butter, and keep it cool. A slice of this excels all the cream cheese that can be made.

*The Art of Cookery Made Plain and Easy
Hannah Glasse, 1796*

---

*Mrs. Fowler was an ancestress of the Dowager Duchess of Radnor. As a Sponsor of the British National Trust School for Americans, Lady Radnor encourages and welcomes students from all over the world.

The suggestions that follow are excellent ways to use up scraps of cheese and are limited only by the imagination of the cook.

✳ Potted Cheese:
Mrs. Glasse's Excellent "Receipt"

*½ pound Cheddar or Cheshire
  cheese, grated
2 tablespoons or little more soft
  butter*

*1½ ounces Madeira wine
dash of grated mace*

Soften cheese and butter; work together until smooth; add wine and mace. Store in an 8-ounce covered jar in refrigerator until ready to use. Serve with crackers and a juicy tart apple, cut into thin slices.

VARIATION
Using same proportions, work ½ pound bleu cheese with 2 tablespoons butter, adding a little brandy and cayenne pepper or paprika. Serve with fresh pears.

✳ Grated-Cheese Sandwich
Filling

*½ pound Cheddar cheese, grated
1 large dill pickle, grated (Polish
  dill are best)*

*mayonnaise
  and mustard, to taste*

Cheese absorbs moisture upon standing. Mix all ingredients together and put in refrigerator to develop flavor and soften. Spread on thin slices of brown bread.

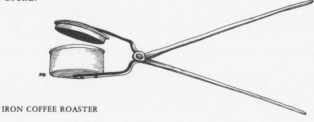

IRON COFFEE ROASTER

✳ Another Sandwich Filling

½ pound Cheddar cheese, grated
1 green onion, chopped fine

3 tablespoons chili sauce
mayonnaise

Mix cheese with green onion and chili sauce, and add enough mayonnaise to moisten. Refrigerate for a day before using.

✳ Fiery Hot Cheese Spread

1 pound mild Cheddar cheese
2 medium-sized onions
1 can (4 ounces) jalapeño peppers,
    seeded

1 cup mayonnaise
little salt

Put cheese, onions and jalapeño peppers through a food chopper, using medium-sized blade. (Be sure to wear rubber gloves when handling jalapeños.) Add mayonnaise and salt, and store in refrigerator. This should be made at least a day ahead of time; improves with age up to about a month. Serve in a crock, with a variety of crackers. *Makes about 3 cups.*

BELLOWS,
STENCIL ON WOOD

✳ Liptauer Cheese Crock

½ pound cream cheese
¼ pound butter
1 tablespoon capers
3 tablespoons sour cream
1 tablespoon paprika

1 tablespoon prepared mustard
1 tablespoon anchovy paste
1 tablespoon minced green onion
½ tablespoon caraway seeds

Soften cream cheese and butter, mash capers, and mix all ingredients together. Keep refrigerated. Serve from a crock, with crackers or chips. *Makes about 2 cups.*

Hors-d'oeuvre were not served in early America, but a number of "favorites" are included below for your enjoyment.

❋ Mushroom Dip

{ *Adapted from "A White Fricasse of Mushrooms,"* The Art of Cookery, 1796 }

4 tablespoons butter
3 tablespoons minced shallots
½ pound mushrooms, sliced thin
2 tablespoons flour
1 cup heavy cream

½ teaspoon salt
⅛ teaspoon cayenne pepper
1 tablespoon minced parsley
½ tablespoon minced chives
½ teaspoon lemon juice

In a heavy 10-inch skillet slowly melt butter and add shallots. Stir constantly over moderate heat for about 4 minutes. Do not let shallots brown. Stir in mushrooms and coat thoroughly with butter. Continue to cook and stir until moisture evaporates, 10 to 15 minutes. Remove skillet from heat. Sprinkle flour over mushrooms and stir until no trace of flour remains. Pour cream over mushrooms and slowly bring to a boil, stirring constantly until mixture thickens. Reduce heat to barest simmer and cook for 2 minutes. Remove skillet from heat; stir in salt, cayenne, parsley, chives and lemon juice. Serve hot in chafing dish, with Melba toast. (Freezes well.) *Makes 2½ cups.*

❋ Oyster Dip

½ pound butter
4 tablespoons margarine
4 bunches of green onions, chopped
    fine
3 celery ribs, chopped fine
1 celery heart, chopped fine
2 small bell peppers, chopped fine

3 pints shelled fresh oysters, with
    liquor
16 wafer-type crackers, crushed
1 teaspoon Worcestershire sauce
½ teaspoon black pepper
4 or 5 drops of Tabasco
⅛ teaspoon garlic salt

Melt butter and margarine in a heavy skillet, and sauté the chopped vegetables slowly until transparent but not brown. Keep covered. Pour in oyster liquor and heat. Add oysters; stir constantly with a large metal spoon, cutting oysters while stirring. Add crushed wafers to absorb liquid. If necessary, add 2 or 3 more wafers. Then add the Worcestershire sauce, black pepper, Tabasco and garlic salt. Stir gently; adjust seasonings. Serve from a chafing dish, with additional crackers for dipping. *Makes 12 to 16 servings.*

1820 GEORGE WASHINGTON BOTTLE, PENNSYLVANIA
1820 SUNBURST BOTTLE, CONNECTICUT

✳ Pickled Shrimps

3 pounds shrimps, cleaned and
   cooked
3 onions, sliced very thin
7 or 8 bay leaves
1¼ cups salad oil
¾ cup white vinegar

½ tablespoon salt
2½ teaspoons celery seeds
2½ tablespoons capers and juice
generous dash of Tabasco
1 garlic clove

Alternate layers of shrimps and onions in a shallow glass dish. Make a marinade of other ingredients and pour over the shrimps. Cover and let stand in refrigerator for 24 hours, or longer, to develop flavor. Remove garlic and bay leaves. Drain shrimps and onions. Serve icy cold on food picks. *Makes 12 to 15 servings.*

✳ Madras Artichokes

1 bite-size artichoke bottom
1-inch square of processed
   American cheese

1-inch square of crisp bacon
½ teaspoon chutney

Assemble in above order on a cookie sheet. Run under the broiler until cheese melts.

    This can be served as a vegetable if larger artichokes are used and other ingredients are increased proportionately. *Makes 1 serving.*

✳ Pâté

{ Adapted from traditional French recipe }

½ pound chicken livers
½ pound soft margarine
⅓ cup dry Vermouth
2 tablespoons minced onion

2 tablespoons minced parsley
1 teaspoon salt
¼ teaspoon minced tarragon
4 eggs

Place all ingredients in a blender and blend at medium speed until everything is well mixed and raw livers have liquefied. Pour into 5 or 6 well-oiled 6-ounce ramekins or a single 4-cup baking dish. Set in a shallow pan containing 1 inch of water. Bake in 325° oven for approximately 30 minutes, or until a knife inserted comes out clean. Time will vary according to size of baking dish. This is a light, custardlike pâté with a sophisticated flavor. Delicious with cold radishes and melba toast. *Makes 5 or 6 servings.*

PETER YOUNG
PEWTER CHALICE

✳ Caviar Canapé

10 slices of firm white bread
6 tablespoons water
1 garlic clove, crushed
6 to 8 tablespoons good olive oil
3 to 4 tablespoons lemon juice

3½ ounces red salmon caviar
¼ cup minced parsley
2 tablespoons minced green onion
tops

Trim crusts from bread slices, and crumble bread well. Sprinkle with the water and squeeze dry. This should pack down to about 1 cup. Add other ingredients and mix well. Adjust olive oil and lemon juice to taste. Pack in a dish or jar and refrigerate for several hours. Serve with crusty French bread or Melba toast. This is good served with radishes, strips of green pepper, ripe olives and a good Alsatian wine. *Makes about 2 cups.*

✳ Cheese Wafers

½ pound sharp cheese, grated fine
¼ pound butter or margarine
1½ cups flour

½ teaspoon paprika
½ teaspoon salt

Work cheese and butter together until blended. Gradually work in the flour, paprika and salt which have been sifted together. Roll out ¼ inch thick and cut into circles the size of a quarter. Bake on a lightly greased cookie sheet in 350° oven for about 15 minutes. Wafers should be crisp but not brown. *Makes 6 to 8 dozen.*

VARIATIONS

1 For a snappier hot cheese wafer, add ½ teaspoon cayenne pepper and 1½ cups unsweetened, crisp rice cereal or finely chopped pecans to the recipe. Mix dough lightly so that the crisp cereal will not disintegrate, and drop by teaspoons onto the cookie sheet. Press with the tines of a fork to flatten.

2 CHEESE-OLIVE PUFFS: Thus dough can be shaped into a roll and cut into slices. Wrap each slice around a stuffed olive to make delicious cheese-pastry-coated olives for *hors-d'oeuvre.*

3 An unusual wafer can be made by using the basic recipe without cayenne pepper; roll each cooked wafer in confectioners' sugar before it has cooled. These are especially good with sherry and for "coffees."

OLIVE AMBER WINE-
SPIRIT BOTTLE, 1700-30

127

✳ Eggplant Caviar

1 large eggplant, about 1½ pounds
¾ cup olive oil
2 onions, chopped fine
*2 or 3 large tomatoes, peeled and
    chopped*

2 garlic cloves, crushed
1 teaspoon minced parsley
salt and pepper

Coat eggplant with oil and bake in 350° oven until tender, about 1 hour. Cool and peel. Chop pulp fine in a large bowl. Add onions, tomatoes and garlic, and chop all together very fine. Add remaining oil, parsley, and salt and pepper to taste. Mix well and chill for several hours before using. Serve with hot buttered thin-sliced toast or mild crackers. *Makes 6 to 8 servings.*

ENGLISH WOODEN MEASURE

Entertainment

Each age has deemed the new-born year.
The fittest time for festal cheer. *Marmion, Sir Walter Scott*

In the interest of merriment and enjoyment, this chapter glances at a variety of ideas which reawaken old customs, celebrations and traditions. In contemplating a party, be it a Christmas feast or a summer picnic, it is important to plan well in advance, allowing ample time to develop a theme and secure all the necessary ingredients. We hope what follows will be of help and will provide today's hostess with enough information to enable her to re-create a meal from out of the past. With these notes as inspiration we suggest the reader add a dash of ingenuity, a pinch of variation, and perhaps a sprinkling of adaptability.

The early seventeenth-century American settlers who had the means were anxious to keep up with fashion. This group probably covered their tables first with a carpet and then with a white linen cloth in anticipation of the dinner meal. Large napkins were placed on the table for each diner along with pewter spoons. Wealthy families used delftware plates and bowls, and their standing salt would have been pewter. Drinking vessels might have been pewter mugs or horn glasses. With the dawn of the eighteenth century, the carpet was done away with. Additional attention

ENGLISH SILVER CANDELABRA,
MATTHEW BOULTON, 1784

was paid to napkins and they were often folded into fanciful shapes, and sometimes small breads were tucked into the folds. Wineglasses were used but not water glasses. The wine or punch was often ceremoniously present- ed in front of the guests. The host, provided with a tumbler, spoon and strainer, made a great production of preparing the drink to the delight of his captive audience. Saltcellars were placed on diagonal corners with crossed serving spoons guarding them, and were beginning to be made in silver. Silver flatware was still in short supply, though forks were available.

By the nineteenth century all classes of society in America possessed knives, forks and spoons, and often in matching sets. Pewter was more common but of course silver was more fashionable. Late-evening dinner parties became popular among the gentry in the cities. Toward the end of the century chic French restaurants sprang up in the large metropolitan areas and it became the custom to entertain away from the home.

Mrs. Janvier, writing in her journal of the 1800s, recalls that after one of her widowed father's dinner parties the ladies retired and the cloth was removed, "together with the undercloth of green baize, which was always used to protect the polished mahogany from the heat of the dishes; and at that juncture the 'Coasters' were called into special use. Having baize on the bottom, they were coasted round the table, with their decanters, with perfect ease and smoothness; while the precious hand-rubbed mahogany derived no harm to its high polish. How often the decanters were replen- ished, while the genial host and his friends sat over the table, this depon- ent sayeth not." Later, the gentlemen rejoined the ladies in the parlor for fruits, biscuits, cakes, tea and coffee.

Actual table ornamentation in the United States did not attain major importance until the Victorian influence took hold. Earlier attempts at decoration seem to have been confined to special occasions. The Colonial Americans sometimes filled shallow tin containers with wet sand; flowers on short stems were tightly packed into the containers. The shape and colors used depended on the theme being represented. Diagrams of the placement of dishes on the dining table during the eighteenth century seem to indicate that plates, eating utensils and napkins were placed on a side table. Diners gathered themselves around the table as best they could, for the table was crowded with bowls, platters, tureens and dishes, carefully arranged in a balanced design. The Victorian table at the height of its splendor provided place settings for each diner, but then proceeded through massive decorations of flowers, fruits and greenery to engulf the poor diners and dwarf the tables. After the Victorian opulence subsided, a restrained elegance developed which more or less continues today.

As mentioned earlier, Colonial living, contrary to some beliefs, offered many opportunities for feasting and merry entertainments. Perhaps the most gala parties of all were provided by the aristocratic families of the Tidewater region of Virginia. Here many of the famous plantations flourished, casting a magic spell which would live on in the minds of romantics long after toasts were given for the last time to the "Sons of America."

These plantation barons closely followed the English fashion. Sons and daughters were sent to England for school, or educated at home by chosen private tutors. One such tutor was Philip Vicker Fithian, a young Princeton University graduate, who became tutor to the Robert Carter children at "Nomini Hall" in 1773. He marvels in his diary at "entertainments" such as boat races, barbecues, fish feasts, horse races, informal dances (which usually followed a visit from the dancing master), and elaborate festivities which lasted for several days. "Nothing is now to be heard of in conversation, but the *Balls*, the *Foxhunts*, the fine *Entertainments*, and the *good fellowship* which are to be exhibited at the approaching Christmas." Mr. Fithian describes dancing to the tune of a French horn and two vio-

ENGLISH SILVER-PLATE WINE COOLER,
MATTHEW BOULTON, 1784

lins. The order of the dances was first minuets, then jugs, reels and, last, "All Country-Dances."

Fox hunting dates from the earliest period in Colonial America, for it was during these pioneer times that the fox was first considered an animal of "the higher chase" in England. Gentlemen of leisure in Virginia, Maryland, Pennsylvania, and on Long Island organized into hunting clubs. Lavish breakfasts were served before the hunt and a suitable feast followed the day's chase. People often think of the hunt breakfast as the beginning of buffet-style dining in America. This may not have been the case, for legend suggests that credit for the introduction of buffet dining in America goes to Benjamin Franklin. While he served as Ambassador to France (1776-1785), he enjoyed this French method of serving food for large gatherings.

Great attention and careful planning went into all Southern entertainments. An unpublished diary by Mrs. Charles T. Picton (Lida G. Means) describes her memories of Alabama living in the first half of the nineteenth century. The daughter of a prosperous planter, she describes a dinner party as follows: "These dinners began with soup—okra if in season—ham, turkey or chicken, or mutton, every vegetable of the season, pastries of various sorts, or other desserts, and melons, peaches, figs, apricots, nectarines and grapes, if in season, and a few homemade wines." Even on hot summer days these meals, which were served during the heat of the day, always lasted two hours.

One more item is of particular interest in Mrs. Picton's diary. It reflects on a remembered family wedding, "First thing to be done was to prepare the sugar for icing the cake. There was no pulverized sugar then. The loaves of sugar had to be broken into small pieces, rolled as fine as possi-

AMERICAN SILVER PITCHER, ADOLF HIMMEL,
NEW ORLEANS, 1850

ENGLISH GEORGIAN STOP-FLUTED
SILVER CANDLESTICK

ble, sifted." Then it was rubbed through a doubled veiling again and
again. Cakes were baked a week in advance. "Aunt Juliet" had learned
"trimming and ornamenting" from a confectioner in Mobile. It was a
large wedding; "Fifty cakes were baked in Dutch ovens on the hearth,
with coals of fire, by one cook and not one burned." Round and square
pyramids of cake were baked in graduated tins. As a substitute for cake
stands, between the layers small round pieces of wood with three legs 3
inches long were used. They were trimmed with white paper fringed and
pasted on the wood. The day after the wedding, there was a huge dinner
of ham, turkey, chickens, salad, cakes and ice cream for the remaining
wedding party.

A popular late-evening party during the mid-Colonial period was a
"Rout." The dress was formal and guests came to dance and play cards,
and to be treated to a dessert table that was a work of art. The mistress of
the house assisted in the kitchen preparing "little devices" to ornament the
cakes. Swags of icing were used along with candied violets and paper
cupids and birds. The candlesticks flickered soft light over creams, jellies,
ice creams, ices, cookies, tarts, sweetmeats, nuts, raisins, marzipan fruits
and a frothy syllabub.

Mrs. Janvier's unpublished diary describes in full detail the table setting
of a late eighteenth-century, affluent Philadelphian's dinner party: "At
each of the four corners (if they could be called 'corners' when the long
table was oval) stood a high silver-framed openwork salt cellar with the
glass inside. They were mounted on little claw feet, and the glass was dark
blue. Silver tablespoons were laid at each side of them, besides others at
different parts of the table. The silver castors, now but seldom seen, stood
in the middle of the table and 'Canton mats' mathematically placed all
round. The dishes and plates were of blue Canton china. . . .

"The knives and forks had green ivory handles. Our glass decanters of different wines, principally Madeira, stood in silverplated 'coasters'— The wine glasses were of a different shape from those now in use, and the water was in glass carafes. There was much beautiful cut glass in use, . . . and the tumblers were of a very pretty shape."

Thanksgiving feasts have changed little since Colonial times, and the dependable sameness of this festive family gathering establishes its sincerity and charm. A Massachusetts diary (1797) describes a Thanksgiving dinner including fowls and roast pork or spareribs, plum pudding, three kinds of pies—mince, apple and pumpkin.

We all long for an old-fashioned Christmas, with the coziness and mellow thoughts it evokes. When planning an authentic early-American Christmas, one would have to realize that the early New England settlers did not observe this holiday. A 1659 law outlawed "paganistic" Christmas merrymaking in Puritan New England. A few Church of England colonists in Massachusetts did observe Christmas traditions, the Yule log, and traditional foods such as plum pudding and mince pies, and a wassail punch. Christmas did not become a legal holiday in Massachusetts until 1856.

The middle and southern colonies were of a different spirit. With the emphasis on celebrating the coming of the New Year and the rekindling of old-world traditions, much feasting and merrymaking resulted. The Dutch Yuletide observance featured "St. Nicholas" with his long Dutch pipe and broad-brimmed hat. In America he was given short pants and became jolly and plump. Through British influence, St. Nicholas Day merged with the Virginia Christmas which Captain John Smith knew. Here everyone enjoyed the delights of Christmas with bell ringing, Yule log burning, the ever-present feasting, dancing, games and carol singing. Homes were decorated with swags of evergreens, apples and nuts, and dining rooms sparkled with all the table finery a family owned. In the South, greetings were sent to neighbors by setting off firecrackers or firearms. "Old Christmas" often was observed to commemorate the visit of the Magi on January 6 or 7, and a traditional evening dessert party marked this Twelfth Night occasion.

The first American "Christmas trees" were set up by the Hessian soldiers during the Revolution, but it was almost 100 years before the fir tree took its place of honor as a vital part of Christmas in America. The early tree decorations were tufts of cotton, cranberries and popcorn strings, candles clipped on in tin holders, various shapes and chains in colored paper, gilded nut shells and candy canes.

Traditional food at Christmas in America has changed little. The roast turkey has always been a favorite. France seems to be the only other country so honoring the turkey. Cranberries, which had been introduced to the colonists by the Indians, were used in sauces, jellies and tarts. Plum pudding and mince pies were expected, as was a steaming bowl of wassail. The Moravians baked delicious thin cookies in various animal shapes

HESTER BATEMAN SILVER
AND CRYSTAL CRUET SET

(often hung on their Christmas trees), and they made mint and sugar cakes to share with their friends.

Mrs. Janvier recalls (in the Pennsylvania country houses in the late eighteenth century): "At Christmas time there were no shops to go to for purchasing presents and no festivities of any kind that were practicable; but the friendly woods were resorted to, as on many other occasions, and hemlock, pine, and holly, full of berries, were brought home and arrayed about the pictures and long gilt-framed looking-glass extending the whole width of the mantelpiece.

"On the day before Christmas, my sisters . . . and I . . . had to crack both walnuts and shellbarks, to polish the handsomest red and yellow apples, and to make some of the red ones into candlesticks, by cutting a hole at the blossom end, of a proper size to be fitted with a tiny candle. Several of these lent their modest aid in adding to the brilliancy of the larger lights in high candlesticks on the table.

"The silver-plated cake basket was filled with different kinds of cake already made for Christmas, and gingerbread and doughnuts were served in handsome china dishes, while cut glass dishes were used for the nuts.

"Cider was supplied (from apples in our own orchard) in cut glass decanters, and water in goblets—These vessels stood each in its own silverplated 'coaster'—The best we had in the sideboard, in the way of china and silver, was paraded that night."

A description left by an unidentified Southern lady describes Christmas feasting around 1850, bringing to mind a veritable orgy in eating. There was "turkey upon turkey, until the hounds were languid over the turkey bones," a special four- or five-year-old smoked ham, and a spiced beef round in a crust accompanied by a garnish of pickled cucumbers. A pyramid of jellied apples decorated the center of the table. These were considered more of a delicacy than the common cranberry to complement the turkey. No mention is made of vegetables, but the ever-present corn bread seems to have been the preferred bread though "finicky persons ate biscuits or light bread."

IRON TWO-PIECE "LAMB" CAKE MOLD

As expected in the South, baking was of prime importance. "Mammy" baked the pound cakes, cheesecakes, fried pies and sweet-potato custard (baked in crusts and served hot or cold). "We had fancy cakes aplenty— silver cake, gold cake, marble cake—but Mammy sniffed scorn of them and left their making to the white folks." Mammy did make snowballs, however, which were small pound cakes baked in deep coffee cups and then heavily frosted. These were clustered invitingly around a bowl of syllabub, a pyramid of apples or basket of fruits. A boiled batter pudding (a bland pudding with raisins) seems to have been preferred over the traditional plum pudding, which was prepared only "when we felt we must live up fully to English Christmas traditions." Coffee was served with dinner and sweet wine after, accompanied by pineapple or Stilton cheese, both well laced in advance with good brandy. "Yet after such eating and drinking it was nothing to gallop ten miles, dance from eight until day-break—and come home fresh as a rose."

In New York in the 1970s the New Year's Day partygoer sips a Bloody Mary and watches football on TV. In the mid-1800s, a Dutch custom prevailed in that city: the ladies dressed in their finest and re-mained at home. The gentlemen went calling and were greeted by the la-dies, who presided over an assortment of oysters, cakes, preserves, wines and hot coffee. Old grudges were to be forgotten and forgiven merely by making a visit to a person's house on this occasion.

For a final party suggestion the following is offered. Your three au-thors, two native Texans and one transplanted, could not close without at least one "Tall Texas Tale."

In 1835 Herman Ehrenberg, a young German who fought with the New Orleans Greys during the Texas Revolution, left this account of a banquet given for the Greys in Nacogdoches shortly before the company set out for the battlefields: "At the hour appointed for the celebration, col-onists and volunteers crowded around a long, narrow table made of boards. . . . In the midst of our table there stood a large black bear, nicknamed Mr. Petz. This huge creature, which was the main dish of our menu, was so skillfully dressed in his fur that he seemed to be still alive; his mouth was drawn back in a fierce grin and showed sharp, white teeth tightly holding the true colors of the 1824 constitution. Raccoons, opossums, squirrels, and turkeys surrounded Mr. Petz, while two large legs of mutton, roasted to a nice brown, and a substantial joint of beef completed the decoration of our board. . . ." Soon the skin was stripped from "Mr. Petz who, brown and roasted, looked much more attractive than when he wore his bristling, furry coat." The banquet continued with toasts and political talk until finally each guest "returned to his bed with thoughts of the Revolution whirling in his brain and inexhaustible courage welling up from his heart."

❀ Baked Indian Pudding

Indian pudding is good baked. Scald a quart of milk (skimmed milk will do,) and stir in seven table spoonfuls of sifted Indian meal, a teaspoonful of salt, a teacup of molasses, and a great spoonful of ginger, or sifted cinnamon. Baked three or four hours. If you want whey, you must be sure and pour in a little cold milk after it is all mixed.

The American Frugal Housewife
Mrs. Child, 1836

* Olde-Tyme Indian Pudding

{ *Adapted from "Baked Indian Pudding,"* The American Frugal Housewife, *1836* }

1 ⅔ cups milk
5 tablespoons cornmeal
2 tablespoons butter
2 eggs, well beaten

1 cup dark molasses
1 teaspoon salt
1 teaspoon ground cinnamon
¼ teaspoon ground ginger

Scald 1 cup of the milk in the top part of a double boiler over boiling water. Add cornmeal and butter, then remove from heat to let cool for 25 minutes. Meanwhile beat eggs and add to molasses with salt, cinnamon and ginger. Mix thoroughly with the cooled milk and meal mixture. Pour into a buttered deep 1-quart dish and pour remaining 2/3 cup cold milk over it. Bake in 350° oven for 1 hour and 10 minutes. Allow pudding to sit for 20 minutes before serving, for liquid to be partially reabsorbed. Adding the 2/3 cup of milk at the end will result in having an inch of clear liquid at the bottom of the dish. Serve with vanilla ice cream. *Makes 6 servings.*

✳ Quaker Bread Pudding

{ *Adapted from "Bread Pudding,"* The American Frugal Housewife, *1836* }

2 cups milk	*2 eggs*
4 tablespoons butter	*⅛ teaspoon salt*
⅔ cup sugar	*½ teaspoon grated nutmeg*
4 cups cubes of stale bread	*1 teaspoon vanilla extract*
½ cup raisins	

Scald milk and add butter and sugar. Stir until butter has melted and sugar has dissolved. Pour over the bread and raisins and let stand for 20 to 30 minutes. Beat the eggs well with salt, nutmeg and vanilla. Add to bread mixture. Pour into a well-buttered 1½-quart dish, and bake in 350° oven for 35 to 45 minutes. *Makes 6 servings.*

✳ Vanilla Ice Cream

{*Adapted from "Vanilla Cream,"* The Virginia Housewife, *1824*}

1 tablespoon cornstarch	*2 cups heavy cream*
¾ cup sugar	*¼ teaspoon salt*
2 eggs, separated	*1 tablespoon vanilla extract*
2 cups milk, scalded	

Mix cornstarch, sugar and egg yolks well. Add scalded milk slowly and cook until mixture reaches the boiling point. Cool. Add cream, salt and vanilla. Beat egg whites stiff and fold in. Freeze in a crank ice-cream freezer or in the refrigerator. If in refrigerator, stir and blend well several times during freezing to keep smooth. *Makes 1½ quarts.*

VARIATIONS

1 Add 2 tablespoons instant coffee powder with 2 tablespoons brandy.

2 Soak ½ cup raisins in ½ cup rum. Add, with 1 cup chopped pecans and finely shredded rind of 1 lemon.

3 Add 1 cup crumbled macaroons and 1/3 cup sherry.

❋ Apricot Ice

2 cups sugar
2 rounded tablespoons flour
6 cups water
juice of 4 oranges

juice of 2 lemons
3 cans (16 ounces each) peeled apricots

In a large kettle cook the sugar, flour and water until syrup is clear. Cool. Add orange and lemon juice together with apricots which have been well mashed (or puréed in a blender) with their juice. Freeze in a hand freezer for smoothest consistency. If freezing in refrigerator, let freeze until about half-frozen, then remove and beat with electric mixer until smooth; return to freezer. Remove and beat again just before ice is firm; return to freezer. *Makes about 3 quarts.*

VARIATION
Greengage plums are delicious in place of the apricots.

LATE GEORGIAN SILVER WINE
FUNNEL; EARLY 19TH CENTURY
DECANTER AND GLASS

✳ Cold Chocolate Soufflé

*2 ounces (2 squares) unsweetened
chocolate, melted
½ cup confectioners' sugar
1 cup milk, heated
1 envelope unflavored gelatin
¼ cup cold water*

*¾ cup granulated sugar
1 teaspoon vanilla extract
¾ teaspoon salt
2 cups heavy cream, whipped
grated unsweetened chocolate for
topping*

Combine 2 ounces chocolate and the confectioners' sugar in a saucepan. Gradually add hot milk, stirring constantly. Place over low heat and stir until mixture reaches the boiling point, but do *not* boil. Remove from heat and stir in gelatin that has been softened in the cold water. Add granulated sugar, vanilla and salt; mix thoroughly. Chill until slightly thickened, then beat until light and fluffy. Fold in whipped cream, and chill for 2 to 3 hours, or until set. Before serving, grate unsweetened chocolate over the top. (Can be made 2 or 3 days in advance and kept covered in refrigerator.) *Makes 6 to 8 servings.*

SHEFFIELD SILVER-PLATE
DOUBLE WINE SLIDE

✳ Lemon Flummery

*{ Adapted from "Flummery," The Virginia Housewife,
1824 }*

*1 cup boiling water
1 package (3 ounces) lemon-
flavored gelatin
¾ cup dry sherry or white wine*

*¼ cup heavy cream
½ cup sweetened whipped cream
for topping*

Add boiling water to gelatin and stir to dissolve gelatin completely. Add sherry and ¼ cup cream. Mix thoroughly and pour into five 4-ounce serving molds. Chill to set. When ready to serve, top with whipped cream. *Makes 5 servings.*

✳ Basic Fruit Mousse

1 package (3 ounces) fruit-flavored
gelatin
½ cup boiling water
1 envelope unflavored gelatin
¼ cup cold water
2 cups mixed fruit juice and puréed
fruit

2 tablespoons lemon juice
2 tablespoons grated lemon rind
1 cup heavy cream
3 egg whites
⅛ teaspoon salt
3 to 6 tablespoons sugar

Use the same flavor of gelatin as fruit juice and fruit. Dissolve fruit-flavored gelatin in the boiling water. Soften unflavored gelatin in the cold water, and add to hot gelatin, stirring until all is thoroughly dissolved. Add puréed fruit mixture, lemon juice and rind. Allow mixture to chill until it begins to set. Remove from refrigerator and beat until light and fluffy. Whip the heavy cream to soft peaks and fold in. Taste to correct sweetness. (If more sugar is needed, it can be folded in with egg whites.) Beat egg whites with salt until they hold stiff peaks, adding as much of the sugar as needed. Fold into basic mixture gently. Turn into a 2-quart ring mold or soufflé dish, and let set in refrigerator for several hours. Serve with sweetened whipped cream. *Makes 8 to 10 servings.*

VARIATIONS

1 STRAWBERRY MOUSSE: 2 cups sweetened frozen strawberries puréed in blender; omit lemon juice and use only 1 tablespoon grated rind. Decorate with candied violets.

2 ORANGE MOUSSE: 1 cup frozen orange-juice concentrate and 1 cup water. Flavor with 3 to 4 tablespoons Cointreau, and decorate with Mandarin orange sections and fresh mint sprigs.

3 APRICOT MOUSSE: 2 cups canned apricot halves puréed with a little of the syrup. Decorate with finely chopped crystallized gingerroot.

4 GREENGAGE MOUSSE: 2 cups greengage plums puréed with a little of the syrup. Decorate with candied rose petals.

The variety of combinations is endless, as are the flavorings: almond, rum, Cointreau, Cherry Heering, Kirsch, etc. When flavoring with liqueur, reduce the amount of lemon juice and rind. Let your own taste dictate the flavor combinations.

ENGLISH PEWTER CHARGER

✳ Clarice's Floating Island

{ *Adapted from "Apple Souffle,"* Grosvenor, 1850 }

2 heaping tablespoons cornstarch
4 cups milk
6 egg yolks, beaten

1 cup sugar
⅛ teaspoon salt
1 teaspoon vanilla extract

Dissolve cornstarch in 1 cup of the milk and add to beaten egg yolks, sugar and salt. In top part of a double boiler scald remaining 3 cups milk. Add egg mixture to scalded milk, and stir continually over boiling water until mixture is. thick but not firm. This custard does not thicken as it cools. Cool, add vanilla. Spoon into a flameproof serving bowl.

FLOAT
3 egg whites   ½ teaspoon vanilla extract
3 tablespoons sugar

Beat egg whites until stiff but not dry. Add sugar a little at a time, then vanilla. When custard is cool, skim off any "crust" and spread float carefully on top. Run under the broiler to brown tips of meringue. *Makes 8 to 10 servings.*

✳ Trifle

{ *Adapted from "To Make a Trifle,"* The Art of Cookery, 1796 }

2½ cups vanilla custard
1 sponge cake (8 ounces) sliced, or
   24 ladyfingers
¾ to 1 cup medium sherry
8 ounces raspberry jam

¾ cup candied cherries, sliced
¾ cup toasted sliced almonds
1 cup heavy cream
3 tablespoons sugar
½ teaspoon vanilla extract

Make thin vanilla custard; if you use a packaged mix, add ½ cup extra milk. In your best 2-quart crystal bowl, arrange a layer of sponge cake or ladyfingers on the bottom, and line the sides. Sprinkle with ½ cup sherry. Pour half of custard over cake. Dot with raspberry jam, half of candied cherries, and one third of almonds. Arrange another layer and repeat, saving out 12 cherry halves for decoration. Whip the cream, sweeten with sugar, and flavor with vanilla. Spread enough to cover over the top of the trifle, and decorate with cherry halves. Serve rest of cream in a small bowl. *Must* be made 6 to 8 hours before serving. *Makes 6 to 8 servings.*

✳ Tante's Grape Mousse Parfait

20 large marshmallows   *2 cups whipped cream*
½ cup grape juice

With scissors cut marshmallows into quarters. Place grape juice and cut marshmallows in a saucepan, and stir constantly over low heat until marshmallows melt. Remove from heat and allow to cool. When beginning to set, gently fold in whipped cream. Spoon into parfait glasses and chill for at least 4 hours. A tiny bit of additional whipped cream may be added on top for color contrast. This amount, about 1 tablespoon, could be taken from the 2 cups called for in the recipe. *Makes 6 servings.*

VARIATION
Use ½ cup prepared double-strength coffee instead of grape juice, to make coffee parfait.

CUT CRYSTAL WINE RINSE

✳ Hot Apricot Soufflé

1 cup sherry-soaked dried apricots, *5 egg yolks*
 with liquid   *6 egg whites*
1 cup sugar   *½ pint French vanilla ice cream*
½ teaspoon salt   *additional Cognac or liqueur*
⅓ cup Cognac or apricot liqueur

Blend the apricots and any remaining soaking liquid, sugar, salt, 1/3 cup Cognac and the egg yolks in a blender. Beat egg whites until stiff but not dry, and fold into mixture. Pour into a buttered and sugared 1½-quart soufflé dish. Bake in 400° oven for 25 to 28 minutes. Serve hot, with a sauce made of softened vanilla ice cream mixed with a little Cognac or other liqueur used in the soufflé. *Makes 4 to 6 servings.*

✽ Charlotte Russe

{ Adapted from "Charlotte d'Russe most excellent,"
Grosvenor, *1850 }*

1 envelope unflavored gelatin
¼ cup cold water
3 eggs, separated
½ cup plus 2 tablespoons sugar
2 cups milk
½ cup sherry

¼ teaspoon salt
2 cups whipped cream
additional whipped cream for
  garnish
grated blanched almonds or shaved
  semisweet chocolate

Soften gelatin in cold water. Beat egg yolks slightly and add ½ cup sugar and the milk. Cook yolks and sugar in top part of double boiler over boiling water to custard stage, and add softened gelatin, beating until dissolved. Remove from heat and add sherry, beating well. Cool. Beat egg whites until foamy, and add salt and 1 tablespoon sugar. Continue beating and add another 1 tablespoon sugar. Beat until peaks just curl over. Fold into cooled custard mixture. Fold 2 cups whipped cream into custard and pour into a fancy 2-quart mold. Chill to set. Invert on a serving platter and garnish with additional whipped cream, and grated almonds or shaved chocolate. *Makes 6 servings.*

BLUE CANTON WARE
CHINESE EXPORT PLATE

✽ Adela's Flan

{ Similar to "Mrs. Fisher's Custards," Grosvenor,
1850 }

1¾ cups sugar
4 cups milk

8 cinnamon sticks
4 eggs, beaten

Melt ¾ cup of the sugar in a small saucepan and cook until caramelized. Pour a small amount of this "burnt" sugar into the bottom of 12 custard cups or small ramekins; 1 teaspoon in each is plenty.

In a large deep heavy skillet cook the milk, remaining 1 cup sugar and cinnamon sticks. Cook over low heat, slowly adding the well-beaten eggs to the milk. Using a cup or ladle, gently pour milk-egg mixture on top of burnt sugar. Set custard cups in a large pan with 1 inch of water in it. Bake in 350° oven for about 35 minutes, or until custard tests done with a knife. Watch constantly so that water in bottom pan does *not* boil. (Add ice cubes if water does boil.) Remove pan from oven but leave custard cups in water in the pan until they reach room temperature.

Serve at room temperature or cold. If serving cold, hold custard cup in warm water for a few seconds before inverting to turn custard out onto individual serving dishes or plates. The caramelized sugar forms a sauce over the inverted custard. *Makes 12 servings.*

❋ Swedish Cream

2 ⅓ cups light cream or half-and-
   half
1 cup sugar

1 envelope unflavored gelatin
2 cups sour cream
1 teaspoon vanilla extract

Heat the cream, sugar and gelatin together over low heat until the sugar and gelatin have dissolved. Fold in the sour cream and vanilla. Pour into 8 individual dishes such as *pots de crème*, stemmed wineglasses, etc. Chill for several hours. Serve alone, or with sugared strawberries, peaches, grapes or other fruits that are happy with sour cream. *Makes 8 servings.*

❋ Almond Crème Brûlée

{ *Adapted from "To Make Almond Cream,"* The Art of Cookery, *1796* }

3 cups heavy cream
6 tablespoons granulated sugar
6 egg yolks
½ teaspoon almond extract

pinch of salt
4½ ounces blanched whole
   almonds, toasted
½ cup light brown sugar

Heat cream in a heavy saucepan. Add granulated sugar and stir until dissolved. Beat egg yolks until light and creamy. Add the hot cream to the egg yolks gradually, whipping constantly with a wire whisk, not an electric beater. Stir in remaining ingredients except the brown sugar. Pour into a 6-cup soufflé dish, and sprinkle brown sugar on top. Bake at 325° for 45 minutes, or until custard tests done. *Makes 6 servings.*

A NOTE ON CAKES

In the cake recipes that follow there are no servings given. A cake for 12 portions served by itself might easily serve 20 portions when accompanied with ice cream, fruit, or sauce. These portions are therefore only a guide.

8-inch-square cake pan: 12 pieces, 2 x 2½ inches

9-inch-square cake pan: 12 pieces, 2¼ x 3 inches

9-inch round layer-cake pans: 8 wedge-shaped pieces

9 x 5 loaf pan: 9 pieces, 1 inch thick

8-inch round tube pan: 12 wedge-shaped pieces

9-inch round tube pan: 14 wedge-shaped pieces

10-inch tube or bundt pan: 16 wedge-shaped pieces

10 x 17 jelly-roll pan: 10 to 12 slices of rolled cake

10-inch springform pan: 10 to 12 pieces

✳❀✳ *Pound Cake*

Wash the salt from a pound of butter, and rub it till it is soft as cream—have ready a pound of flour sifted, one of powdered sugar, and twelve eggs well beaten; put alternately into the butter, sugar, flour, and the froth from the eggs—continuing to beat them together till all the ingredients are in, and the cake quite light: add some grated lemon peel, a nutmeg, and a gill of brandy; butter the pans, and bake them. This cake makes an excellent pudding, if baked in a large mould, and eaten with sugar and wine. It is also excellent when boiled, and served up with melted butter, sugar and wine.

The Virginia Housewife: or, Methodical Cook
Mrs. Mary Randolph, 1824

✳ Pound Cake

{ Adapted from "Pound Cake," The Virginia Housewife, 1824 }

2 cups sugar
2 cups flour
½ pound butter

5 eggs
1 teaspoon each of lemon, rum
    and vanilla extracts

Have all ingredients at room temperature. Preheat oven to 325°. Grease a 9-inch tube or bundt pan generously. Mix all ingredients at one time in a mixer and beat for about 10 minutes, or until smooth. Turn into greased pan. Bake at 325° for about 1 hour, until cake tests done.

NOTE
As in the original, there is no liquid or baking powder or baking soda.

ENGLISH SILVER SPOON WARMER

✳ Apricot Brandy Pound Cake

½ pound butter
3 cups sugar
6 eggs
3 cups flour
¼ teaspoon baking powder
½ teaspoon salt
1 cup sour cream

½ teaspoon light rum
1 teaspoon orange extract
¼ teaspoon almond extract
½ teaspoon lemon extract
1 teaspoon vanilla extract
½ cup apricot brandy

Cream butter and sugar. Add eggs, one at a time, beating thoroughly after each addition. Sift together flour, baking powder and salt. Mix sour cream with all flavorings and apricot brandy. Add flour mixture and sour-cream mixture alternately to butter mixture. Bake in a greased and floured 10-inch bundt pan in 325° oven for about 1 hour and 15 minutes, or until a wooden pick inserted comes out clean. Watch carefully after 1 hour.

✻ Chocolate Pound Cake

2 cups sugar
1 cup shortening
4 eggs
2 teaspoons vanilla extract
2 teaspoons butter flavoring
1 cup buttermilk

3 cups flour
½ teaspoon baking soda
1 teaspoon salt
4 ounces German sweet chocolate,
  melted

Cream sugar and shortening. Add eggs, flavorings and buttermilk. Sift dry ingredients and add, then add melted chocolate; blend well. Bake in 9-inch tube pan or bundt pan that has been well greased and sprinkled with sugar. Bake in 300° oven for about 1½ hours. Cover cake tightly when done until it cools.

CUT CRYSTAL FINGERBOWL

These modern liquid shortening cakes have been inspired by nineteenth-century fruit loaf cakes.

✻ Carrot Loaf Cake

2 cups sugar
4 eggs
1½ cups vegetable oil
3 cups flour
2 teaspoons baking soda

2 teaspoons ground cinnamon
pinch of salt
⅓ cup buttermilk or sour milk
3 cups grated carrots
1 teaspoon lemon extract

Beat together sugar and eggs. Blend in oil, mixing well. Sift together the flour, baking soda, cinnamon and salt. Add alternately with buttermilk and mix well. Stir in grated carrots and lemon extract. Pour into 2 well-greased loaf pans (9 x 5 inches). Bake at 300° for about 1½ hours, or until a wooden pick inserted in middle comes out clean. Remove cake from oven, and immediately pour over it, while still in pan, the following syrup.

ORANGE SYRUP

1 cup sugar   *1 teaspoon grated orange rind*
½ cup orange juice

Mix together over medium heat until sugar dissolves. Pour over cake as it comes from the oven.

This cake can be baked in a 10-inch tube pan, well greased and sugared or floured. It will take a little longer to bake.

✳ Pumpkin cake

3 cups sugar
½ tablespoon salt
¾ teaspoon ground allspice
1 teaspoon grated nutmeg
2 teaspoons baking soda
3½ cups flour
4 eggs

⅔ cup water
2 cups cooked mashed pumpkin
   (canned if desired)
1 cup vegetable oil
1 cup chopped nuts or raisins
   (optional)

Sift dry ingredients together. Mix eggs, water, pumpkin and oil. Gradually mix in dry ingredients, blending well. Add nuts or raisins. Turn into a well-greased and sugared 10-inch tube pan, or 2 loaf pans (9 x 5 inches). Bake at 350° for 1 hour, or less time for loaf pans.

✳ Prune Cake

1 cup vegetable oil
2¼ cups sugar
2 teaspoons each of ground
   cinnamon, allspice and cloves
2 teaspoons grated nutmeg
3½ teaspoons vanilla extract
2 cups sifted flour

1 teaspoon baking soda
¾ teaspoon salt
3 eggs
1 cup buttermilk
1 cup puréed prune pulp or baby-
   food prunes
1½ cups chopped pecans

Combine oil, sugar, spices and vanilla in a large mixing bowl; mix well. Sift flour with baking soda and salt and add to oil mixture alternately with eggs and buttermilk. Beat for about 2 minutes. Stir in prune purée and pecans, mixing thoroughly. Turn into a well-greased and sugar-dusted 10-inch tube pan. Bake at 350° for 1 hour.

This cake was developed near New Braunfels, Texas, by transplanted Germans. While it uses American ingredients, the recipe is traditional German.

✳ Fruit-Nut Loaf

3 pounds dates, chopped	1 teaspoon salt
1½ pounds candied pineapple, chopped	12 eggs
	3 cups sugar
1 bottle (8 ounces) maraschino cherries with syrup	4 teaspoons vanilla extract
	3 cups flour
3 pounds pecans, broken into pieces	2 tablespoons baking powder
1 cup bourbon whiskey	

Mix fruits including cherry syrup, pecans, bourbon and salt, and let stand overnight. Next day, beat eggs and sugar until lemony. Add vanilla, and gradually add flour and baking powder which have been mixed together. Add fruit mix and blend well. Pour into loaf pans (9 x 5 inches) which have been well greased and lined with wax paper. Cover with foil. Bake at 325° for 1 to 1½ hours. Pour additional bourbon over finished cakes and wrap well to season for about 1 month.

✳ Mrs. Pipiess' Coffee Cake

{ *from the 1800s diary of Rachel L. King* }

½ pound butter	½ teaspoon salt
1 cup sugar	2 teaspoons ground cinnamon
2 eggs	½ tablespoon ground cloves
1 cup molasses	2 teaspoons vinegar
3 cups flour	1 cup prepared cold strong coffee
1 teaspoon baking soda	½ to ¾ cup raisins (optional)

Cream the butter and sugar together until light and fluffy. Add eggs, one at a time, then molasses. Blend thoroughly. Sift together the flour, baking soda and salt. Soak spices in the vinegar. Add spices and vinegar to sugar-egg mixture and then add, alternately, the coffee and the flour mixture. Fold in raisins. Butter and flour a 10-inch tube or bundt pan. Pour on batter and bake in 325° oven for about 50 minutes.

✳ Gingerbread

{ Adapted from "Mrs. Bush's Good Molasses Gingerbread," Grosvenor, 1850 }

¼ cup dark brown sugar
1 egg
½ cup sour milk (see Note)
1 cup dark molasses
2 cups flour, sifted
1 tablespoon ground ginger (more if desired)

1 teaspoon baking soda
½ teaspoon salt
5½ tablespoons butter
½ cup candied gingerroot sliced thin
⅓ cup seedless raisins

Mix brown sugar and egg. Add sour milk and molasses. Sift dry ingredients together and add them. Melt butter and add to batter. Do not overbeat. Fold in gingerroot and raisins. Spoon into a greased and floured 8-inch square pan. Bake at 325° for 30 to 35 minutes. Do not overcook!

NOTE
To substitute sweet milk, add 1½ tablespoons white vinegar to 1 cup lukewarm sweet milk and let stand for 10 minutes.

✳ Chocolate Potato Cake

{ Newhaus Family, nineteenth century }

2 cups sugar
¼ pound butter
4 eggs, separated
1 cup riced or strained cold boiled white potatoes
2 ounces (2 squares) unsweetened chocolate, melted over steam

1 teaspoon ground cinnamon
2 cups flour
2 teaspoons baking powder
½ teaspoon salt
½ cup milk
1 cup fine-chopped pecans

Cream sugar and butter well. Add the egg yolks, one at a time, stirring well after each addition. Add potatoes, melted chocolate and cinnamon. Mix flour with baking powder and salt. Add dry ingredients gradually with milk. Add pecans, and last add egg whites, beaten stiff. Bake in a well-buttered and sugared 8-inch springform tube pan in 350° oven for 1 hour. Or bake in two 8-inch-square layer pans for 30 to 35 minutes. Ice with Cousin Ilse's Chocolate Icing (recipe follows).

COUSIN ILSE'S CHOCOLATE ICING (*a soft fudgelike icing*)

3 ounces (3 squares) unsweetened
  chocolate
4 tablespoons butter
2 egg yolks

1 cup light cream
3 cups sugar
¼ teaspoon salt
1 teaspoon vanilla extract

Melt chocolate and butter in top part of a double boiler over hot water. Beat egg yolks well. Add cream. Combine sugar, salt, melted chocolate and butter, egg yolks and cream in a heavy saucepan. Bring to a slow boil, stirring only until sugar is dissolved. Boil to the soft-ball stage (234°) is reached but *no longer*. Remove from heat, add vanilla, and beat icing until it is thick and begins to feel "heavy." Spread on cake at once. As this sets rapidly, it is important to work fast. If icing gets too hard before finishing, soften over hot water for a few minutes.

✳ Josie's Feather Cake (*devil's food*)

4 tablespoons shortening
4 tablespoons butter
1 cup granulated sugar
1 cup brown sugar
1 teaspoon vanilla extract
2 eggs, beaten
3 ounces (3 squares) unsweetened
  chocolate

½ cup hot water
2 cups cake flour
¼ teaspoon salt
1 teaspoon baking soda
⅔ cup sweet or sour milk

Cream shortening and butter and both sugars; add vanilla and eggs. Beat until fluffy. Melt chocolate in the hot water. Blend thoroughly and cool. Add to creamed mixture. Add flour, sifted with salt and baking soda, alternately with milk. Beat well after each addition. Spoon into two 9-inch layer-cake pans, greased and lightly floured. Bake at 350° for 30 minutes. Ice with Feather Cake Frosting (recipe follows).

FEATHER CAKE FROSTING

6 tablespoons cocoa powder
6 tablespoons prepared hot coffee
6 tablespoons butter

1 teaspoon vanilla extract
3 cups confectioners' sugar

Dissolve cocoa in coffee, and cool. Add butter and vanilla, and beat until smooth. Add sugar gradually until frosting is of good spreading consistency.

✳ Apple Spice Cake

{ *New England traditional* }

2 cups sifted flour
1 teaspoon baking soda
1 teaspoon salt
1 teaspoon ground cinnamon
½ teaspoon grated nutmeg
¼ teaspoon ground cloves
½ cup shortening

¾ cup brown sugar
2 eggs
1 teaspoon vanilla extract
1 cup grated raw apple
2 tablespoons vinegar plus water to
   make ½ cup
½ cup chopped nuts

Combine flour, baking soda, salt and spices. Blend shortening, brown sugar, eggs and vanilla. Add flour mixture alternately with grated apple and vinegar-water. Stir in nuts. Spread in a buttered and floured loaf pan (9 x 5 inches). Bake at 350° for 1 hour, or until a wooden pick inserted comes out clean.

IRON COOKIE CUTTER

✳ Queen's Cake (*a special holiday cake*)

{ *Adapted from "Queen's Cake," Rachel L. King's early diary, nineteenth century* }

6 eggs
1 ⅔ cups granulated sugar
¾ pound butter, softened
1 cup light brown sugar
3 cups flour
1 tablespoon baking powder
1 teaspoon ground cinnamon

¼ teaspoon ground cloves
1 cup slivered almonds
1 cup dried currants
1 cup candied cherries, halved
½ cup brandy
½ cup sherry

Separate eggs. Beat the whites until they hold stiff peaks, and beat in 2/3 cup granulated sugar; set aside. Beat the egg yolks until thick and yellow (no need to wash the beaters); set aside. Cream softened butter and add remaining cup of granulated sugar and the brown sugar; cream thoroughly. Add egg yolks and mix well. Sift together 2 cups flour, the baking powder, cinnamon and cloves. Toss the almonds and fruits in the third cup of flour, to coat each piece and keep them from sticking together. Add the sifted flour mixture to the egg-butter-sugar mixture, alternately with the brandy and sherry. Mix well and stir in the fruit-nut-flour mixture, mixing well. Fold in the egg whites. Turn into 2 well-buttered loaf pans (9 x 5 inches). Handle gently so that the batter retains its lightness. Bake in 275° oven for about 1 hour and 45 minutes.

✳ Oatmeal Cake

1 ¼ cups boiling water
1 cup 5-minute rolled oats
1 ⅓ cups flour
1 teaspoon baking soda
½ tablespoon salt
1 teaspoon ground allspice

1 teaspoon ground cinnamon
¼ pound butter
1 cup light brown sugar
1 cup granulated sugar
2 eggs, beaten

Mix boiling water and oats and let stand for at least 20 minutes. Meanwhile, sift flour, baking soda, salt, allspice and cinnamon. Cream butter with both sugars until light. Add eggs and beat well. Then alternately mix flour and water-oats mixture with sugar mixture. Bake in a greased 9-inch-square pan at 275° for 1 hour, or until a wooden pick inserted in center comes out clean. When baked, immediately spread with Coconut-Pecan Icing (recipe follows). Then, run cake under broiler for approximately 4 minutes, until icing is golden.

COCONUT-PECAN ICING
4 tablespoons butter
½ cup light brown sugar
2 tablespoons heavy cream

½ cup shredded coconut
½ cup chopped pecans

Cream butter with sugar and cream. Mix in coconut and pecans. Use at once. Good on other cakes too; always broil the cake after icing.

WATERFORD CRYSTAL
STANDING SALT

✳ Poppy-Seed Cake

{ Adapted from "To Make a Rich Seed Cake," The Experienced English Housekeeper, 1794 }

⅓ cup poppy seeds
1 cup buttermilk or sour milk
2½ cups flour, sifted
2 teaspoons baking powder
1 teaspoon baking soda
½ teaspoon salt

½ pound butter
1½ cups plus 3 tablespoons sugar
4 eggs
½ teaspoon vanilla extract
grated rind of 1 orange
½ tablespoon ground cinnamon

Mix poppy seeds and buttermilk together, and let stand in refrigerator for several hours or overnight. Sift together flour, baking powder, baking soda and salt. Cream butter and 1½ cups sugar; beat in eggs, one at a time; beat in vanilla and grated orange rind. Stir in flour mixture alternately with buttermilk mixture in about 4 additions of each, stirring until just smooth. Spoon half of batter into a greased and floured 10-inch bundt pan. Mix remaining sugar and cinnamon together and sprinkle mixture over batter. Pour rest of batter into the pan. Bake in 350° oven for about 1 hour, or until a wooden pick comes out clean. Cool in pan for 15 minutes, then turn out to finish cooling. Cover tightly and let season for a day or two for best flavor.

✳ Peach Dessert Cake

¼ pound butter
½ cup plus ⅓ cup sugar
grated rind of 1 lemon
½ teaspoon vanilla extract
2 eggs, unbeaten
1 cup sifted cake flour

1 teaspoon baking powder
¼ teaspoon salt
4 fresh peaches, sliced
½ teaspoon ground cinnamon
¼ cup chopped walnuts
whipped cream for topping

Cream butter and ½ cup sugar, and beat until light and fluffy. Add lemon rind and vanilla. Add eggs, one at a time, beating well after each addition. Sift flour, baking powder and salt. Add one fourth at a time to the first mixture. Blend well. Pour half of batter into a greased and floured 8-inch-square pan, 2 inches deep. Lay peach slices on top of batter. Top with remaining batter and spread with spatula to cover peaches. Mix 1/3 cup sugar, the cinnamon and walnuts together, and sprinkle on top. Bake at 350° for 35 minutes. Serve hot, warm, or room temperature, topped with whipped cream sweetened with 1 tablespoon sugar and mixed with tiny bits of peach.

CAUTION
Batter is stiff and must be spread gently with rubber spatula. Do not remove from oven too soon. Appearance of topping may make you think cake is done before it is!

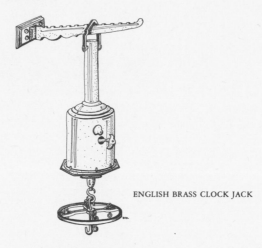

ENGLISH BRASS CLOCK JACK

✳ Sponge Cake

{ *From the 1800s Diary of Rachel L. King* }

6 eggs, separated
1 cup sugar, divided
grated rind of ½ lemon

1 tablespoon lemon juice
1 cup flour
¼ teaspoon salt

Beat egg whites to soft-peak stage. Add ¼ cup sugar slowly, beating constantly. Beat egg yolks until lemony; add lemon rind and juice, and continue beating until thick. Gradually add remaining ¾ cup sugar. Fold both egg mixtures together gently. Sift the flour and salt together and fold into egg mixture. Cook in an ungreased 9-inch tube pan in 325° oven for about 1 hour, cutting through batter several times to remove large air bubbles.

VARIATION
Jelly Roll: Line bottom of buttered jelly-roll pan (10 x 17 inches) with wax paper. Spoon batter evenly into pan and bake at 350° for 10 to 12 minutes. (Use rest of batter for cupcakes, and bake them at 350° for 20 to 30 minutes.) Remove jelly roll to a towel well sprinkled with confectioners' sugar. Pull off paper and trim edges of cake. Roll cake in the

towel and let stand for 5 minutes. Gently unroll, spread with jelly or jam, roll again, and wrap in wax paper. Sprinkle with more confectioners' sugar before serving.

✳ Angel Cake with Sherry or Rum Custard Filling

2 cups milk
¾ cup sugar
4 eggs, well beaten
1 envelope unflavored gelatin
¼ cup cold water

2 cups heavy cream
¼ cup rum or sherry
1 angel-food cake baked in 10-inch
   tube pan
sugar

In top part of a double boiler over boiling water, cook milk, sugar and beaten eggs, stirring constantly, until thick. Soften gelatin in the cold water for 5 to 10 minutes. Add to hot custard and stir for a few minutes. Remove mixture from heat and allow to cool to room temperature. Whip 1 cup of the cream, and add sherry or rum. Fold into custard.

Slice off the top of the angel cake in a ½-inch slice. Scoop out a 2-inch trench all the way around the cake close to the outer rim. This will give you an outside wall, a trench, an inner wall and the original hollow center. The trench should not go through the bottom of the cake. Pour the cooled custard into the trench. Replace cake top and refrigerate overnight. Before serving, whip the remaining cup of cream and sweeten it with 1 or 2 teaspoons of sugar. Cover the cake with the cream and serve.

✳❀✳ *To Make Chacknells*

TO a pound of flour put a pound of butter, six eggs (leaving out the whites), three quarters of a pound of powder-sugar, a glass of water, a little lemon-peel chopped very fine, and dried orange-flowers; work it well together; then cut it into pieces of what bigness you please to bake, and glaze them with sugar.

The Experienced English Housekeeper
Elizabeth Raffald, 1794

✳ **Butter Cookies**

{ Adapted from "To Make Chacknells," The Experienced English Housekeeper, 1794 }

1 pound butter, at room
  temperature
1 cup sugar
2 egg yolks, slightly beaten
grated rind and juice of 1 lemon

2 tablespoons brandy
4½ cups cake flour, sifted
1 teaspoon baking powder
1 egg white, beaten
1 teaspoon light cream

Cream butter (do not use margarine). Add sugar, egg yolks, lemon juice and grated rind, and brandy. Mix well. Work in flour and baking powder which have been sifted together. Dough can be put through a cookie press, or rolled and cut into small rounds, triangles, etc. Glaze with the beaten egg white mixed with the cream. Bake at 350° for 15 minutes.

These cookies keep for weeks and are very successful to decorate at Christmas time. *Makes 6 dozen.*

SHEFFIELD SILVER-PLATE
WINE COASTER, 1770

✳ **Shortbread**

½ pound butter
⅔ cup confectioners' sugar
1 teaspoon vanilla extract

2 cups sifted flour
¼ teaspoon salt

Cream butter with sugar until light. Add vanilla. Sift flour and salt together and add gradually to butter mixture. Shape into a ball and flatten to about 1/3-inch thickness. Place on a cookie sheet and, with a knife, score top in squares. Cut about one third of the depth into dough. Prick all over with a fork. Bake in center of oven at 325° for 25 to 30 minutes, or until lightly browned.

VARIATIONS

1 Shape into small rounds or logs. Bake as usual, but for 12 to 15 minutes.

2 To basic shortbread dough, add ½ cup finely chopped pecans; or ½ cup melted chocolate bits; or ½ cup butterscotch bits. Bake as usual.

✳ Butter Chews (*shortbread variations*)

¼ *pound butter*
¼ *cup confectioners' sugar*
1 *cup flour, sifted*
3 *eggs, separated*

¾ *cup brown sugar*
1 *cup chopped pecans*
¾ *cup flaked coconut*

Mix butter, confectioners' sugar and sifted flour well. Pat in a 9-inch-square pan, lightly greased on bottom and sides, and bake at 350° for 15 minutes. Do not brown. Meanwhile beat egg yolks well and mix with brown sugar, pecans and coconut. Beat egg whites stiff but not dry, and fold yolk mixture into them. Remove cake from oven, and pour the egg mixture over it. Return to the oven, and bake for 30 minutes longer. Cut into squares while warm. *Makes 2 dozen.*

VARIATION
Combine butter, sugar and flour. Bake for 15 minutes. Mix the following ingredients:

2 *eggs, beaten*
1 *cup granulated sugar*

2 *tablespoons lemon juice*
1 *teaspoon grated lemon rind*

Pour evenly over crust and return to oven for 25 minutes. Cool and frost with Lemon Glaze (recipe follows).

LEMON GLAZE
½ *cup confectioners' sugar*
1 *teaspoon lemon juice*

1 *tablespoon water*

Mix sugar, lemon juice and water; add a little more water if too thick to spread easily. Spread thinly over cooled uncut bars.

✳ Marzipan Cookies

{ *Inspired by "To Make March-Pane,"* The Compleat Housewife, *1730* }

¼ *pound butter, softened*
¼ *cup sugar*

⅛ *teaspoon almond extract*
1¼ *cups sifted flour*

Cream butter and sugar until fluffy; add almond extract and blend in flour. Chill. Roll into small balls using about 2 level teaspoons of dough for each, and flatten each one. Bake on an ungreased cookie sheet in top third of 300° oven for about 30 minutes. *Do not brown.* Time will vary with size of cookie.

To make fruit shapes: Use vegetable coloring to color the dough as you wish, i.e., red for apples and cherries; orange for carrots and oranges; yellow for pears and bananas, etc. Shape dough into fruit shapes, using colored food picks for stems, cloves for blossom ends, etc., and bake as above. *Makes 2½ dozen.*

✳ Lebkuchen

{ *German traditional* }

2¾ cups flour
½ teaspoon baking soda
½ teaspoon salt
½ teaspoon each of ground
  cinnamon, cloves and allspice
½ teaspoon grated nutmeg
½ cup honey
½ cup molasses
¾ cup packed light brown sugar

1 egg
1 teaspoon grated lemon rind
1 tablespoon lemon juice
½ cup chopped nuts
¾ cup chopped candied citron
9 dozen blanched almonds
18 candied cherries, halved
Glaze (recipe follows)

Sift flour, measure, and sift again with dry ingredients and spices. Heat together honey, molasses and brown sugar until sugar dissolves. Cool. Stir in egg, lemon rind and juice, and beat in dry ingredients until smooth. Add nuts and citron. Wrap in wax paper and chill overnight.

Roll out dough ¼ inch thick, and cut into 1½-inch squares, approximately. Place on a greased cookie sheet and decorate each square with 3 blanched almonds and ½ candied cherry. Bake at 350° for 12 to 15 minutes. When cakes are done, spread or brush them quickly with glaze. *Makes about 3 dozen.*

SIMPLE GLAZE
1 cup granulated sugar
½ cup water

dash of salt
¼ cup confectioners' sugar

Cook granulated sugar and water together until the syrup spins a thread (215°). Remove from heat, and add salt and confectioners' sugar. Brush on tops of cookies to glaze them, using a pastry brush, or spread on with a spoon.

✳ Fruit Drop Cookies

{ Adapted from "To Make little Currant Cakes," The Experienced English Housekeeper, 1794 }

¼ pound butter
½ cup granulated sugar
½ cup brown sugar
1 egg
1 cup plus 2 tablespoons flour
½ teaspoon salt

½ teaspoon baking soda
1 teaspoon vanilla extract
½ cup nuts
1 cup dried currants or seedless
  raisins

Cream together the butter and both sugars. Add egg and mix. Sift flour, salt and baking soda together, and add to mixture. Stir in vanilla, nuts and currants. Drop on a greased cookie sheet, and bake in 375° oven for 8 to 10 minutes. *Makes 2 to 4 dozen.*

VARIATIONS
Use oatmeal in place of pecans. Use dates, pitted and chopped, in place of currants. Use glacéed chopped fruits in place of raisins, and add ½ teaspoon ground cinnamon and ¼ teaspoon grated nutmeg.

IRISH WATERFORD BUTTER "TUB," 1780

✳ Date-Pecan Cookies

{ Variation of "To Make little Currant Cakes," The Experienced English Housekeeper, 1794 }

4 eggs, separated
1 cup sugar
1 cup flour
2 teaspoons baking powder

pinch of salt
1 pound pecans, chopped
1 pound dates, chopped fine
1 teaspoon vanilla extract

Beat egg yolks and sugar until lemon-colored and fluffy. Add flour, baking powder and salt, mixing well. Then add pecans, dates and vanilla. Beat egg whites stiff and fold in. Drop on a greased cookie sheet in very small pieces, and bake in 350° oven for about 25 minutes. *Makes 6 dozen.*

✳ Oatmeal Crispies

{ Variation of "To Make little Currant Cakes," The Experienced English Housekeeper, 1794 }

1 ½ cups seedless raisins
½ cup shortening
¼ cup water
1 ½ cups 5-minute rolled oats
¾ cup flour
1 cup brown sugar

½ teaspoon baking soda
½ teaspoon salt
¼ teaspoon ground cinnamon
1 teaspoon vanilla extract
½ cup chopped pecans

Combine raisins, shortening and water, and heat until shortening melts. Add rest of ingredients and blend well. Wrap in wax paper and chill in refrigerator for several hours. Grease a cookie sheet. Break off dough in small bits and place bits well apart on cookie sheet. Flatten cookies with the bottom of a glass dipped into sugar. Bake in 350° oven for 8 to 10 minutes. *Makes 4 dozen.*

CHINESE EXPORT PORCELAIN
PUNCH BOWL—"HUNTING" THEME

✳ Sugar Cookies

{ Adapted from "Sugar Cakes," The Art of Cookery, 1796 }

½ pound butter
1 cup sugar
1 egg
2 cups flour

½ teaspoon baking soda
½ teaspoon cream of tartar
pinch of salt
2 teaspoons vanilla extract

Cream butter and sugar, and add egg. Sift dry ingredients together and add to creamed mixture. Add vanilla. Drop pieces of dough as large as walnuts onto an ungreased cookie sheet. Flatten the pieces with the bottom of a glass moistened and dipped into sugar. Bake in 350° oven for 6 to 8 minutes, or until cookies are golden brown on edges. *Makes 5 dozen.*

✳ Meringue Kisses

{ Adapted from "To Prepare Peppermint Drops," A New System of Domestic Cookery, 1807 }

2 egg whites
⅔ cup sugar

½ teaspoon almond extract

Beat egg whites stiff, adding sugar gradually while beating. Beat in almond extract. Drop on a cookie sheet, covered with aluminum foil, in very small spoonfuls to make kisses. Place in oven preheated to 350°; turn off heat at once and leave meringues in oven overnight, with door closed.

VARIATIONS

1 To egg-white and sugar meringues, add 8 ounces chocolate chips, 1 cup chopped pecans and ½ teaspoon vanilla extract.

2 Add 1 cup chopped walnuts and ½ teaspoon rum flavoring.

3 Add 1 teaspoon peppermint flavoring as in the original receipt, and 1 cup crushed peppermint stick candy.

✳ Persimmon Cookies

1 cup persimmon pulp (3 or 4 ripe
  persimmons)
½ cup shortening
1½ cups sugar
2 cups sifted flour
⅛ teaspoon salt
½ teaspoon baking soda

½ teaspoon ground cinnamon
½ teaspoon ground cloves
½ teaspoon grated nutmeg
1 cup chopped nuts
1 cup raisins
1 egg, beaten
1 teaspoon vanilla extract

Put persimmons through food mill or strainer and measure 1 cup pulp. Cream shortening and sugar, and set aside. Combine flour, salt, baking soda and spices, and add to nuts and raisins. Add these to creamed mixture. Stir in persimmon pulp, egg and vanilla. Drop scant teaspoons onto greased cookie sheets. Bake at 375° for 13 to 15 minutes. *Makes about 5 dozen.*

TOWLE BLOSSOM CONTAINER,
HEART SHAPED, 1850

✳ Tat's Chocolate Cookies

2 ounces (2 squares) unsweetened
  chocolate
½ cup shortening
1 cup sugar
2 eggs

1¼ cups flour
1 teaspoon vanilla extract
½ tablespoon brandy
¾ cup chopped pecans

Melt chocolate. Cream shortening and sugar. Add eggs and chocolate. Mix well. Add half of the flour, then vanilla and brandy, then remaining flour. Grease a cookie sheet (or several) well and spread the batter on it in a very thin layer. Press pecans over top into batter. Bake in 350° oven for 15 minutes. Cut into squares and remove from pan at once. *Makes 4 to 5 dozen.*

✳ Helen's Lace Cookies

¼ pound butter
¼ pound margarine
1 cup sugar
2 eggs

1 teaspoon vanilla extract
1 cup quick cooking rolled oats
1 cup chopped pecans
1 teaspoon baking powder

Cream butter and margarine with sugar. Beat in eggs and vanilla. Mix oats, pecans and baking powder, and stir into creamed mixture. Drop by teaspoonfuls onto a well-greased cookie sheet, about 4 inches apart. It is important to place these cookies far apart on the cookie sheet since they spread a great deal during cooking to form a crisp, lacy pattern. Bake in 375° oven for 6 to 10 minutes. *Makes 4 dozen.*

✳ Praline Cookies

⅓ pound butter
½ cup dark molasses
1 cup sugar
2 eggs
½ teaspoon vanilla extract

1¾ cups sifted flour
¼ teaspoon baking soda
¼ teaspoon grated mace
¼ teaspoon salt
2 cups pecans, broken

Melt butter and cool. Add molasses and sugar; mix well. Add eggs and vanilla; beat well. Sift dry ingredients and add to the first mixture, ½ cup at a time, mixing well after last addition. Stir in pecans. Drop scant teaspoons of dough about 2 inches apart, onto a greased and floured cookie sheet. Bake in 375° oven for 10 minutes, and remove from pan immediately. *Makes 5 dozen.*

❀ Macaroone

Blanch a pound of sweet almonds, pound them in a mortar with rose water; whip the whites of seven eggs to a strong froth, put in one pound of powdered sugar, beat it some time, then put in the almonds—mix them well, and drop them on sheets of paper buttered; sift sugar over, and bake them quickly. Be careful not to let them get discolored.

The Virginia Housewife; or, Methodical Cook
Mrs. Mary Randolph, 1824

* Macaroons

{ *Adapted from "Macaroons,"* The Virginia Housewife, *1824* }

½ *pound almond paste*
¾ *cup confectioners' sugar*
½ *teaspoon almond extract*
½ *teaspoon vanilla extract*
2 *egg whites*

generous pinch of salt
1 *tablespoon flour*
¼ *teaspoon baking powder*
granulated sugar

Mix almond paste, confectioners' sugar, almond and vanilla extracts thoroughly with your hands until almond paste has absorbed the sugar. Beat egg whites with salt until foamy but not stiff. Work into paste mixture with flour and baking powder to make a smooth mixture. Drop by teaspoonfuls onto ungreased rice paper. Flatten macaroons with back of wet spoon and sprinkle them with sugar. Allow to stand for 2 to 3 hours. Bake at 300° for 20 minutes, or until light brown. Remove from oven. When cool, moisten paper slightly to remove macaroons. They can be stored in the refrigerator indefinitely. Let them come to room temperature before serving. *Makes about 2½ dozen.*

✳ Apricot Sweetmeats

{ *Adapted from "Apricot Paste,"* The Experienced English Housekeeper, *1794* }

1 pound dried apricots, ground
1½ cups granulated sugar
½ cup orange juice

pecan or walnut halves, or almonds
superfine granulated sugar

Combine apricots, granulated sugar and orange juice in a saucepan. Cook over low heat for 10 minutes, stirring occasionally to prevent sticking. Drop by teaspoon onto wax paper. When cool, place a pecan or walnut half or an almond in the center, rolling apricot mixture around it. Drop each ball into superfine granulated sugar to coat completely. Pack in a tightly covered container to store. *Makes 3 dozen.*

VARIATION
1½ cups sugar
1 pound dried apricots, ground
1 can (3½ ounces) flaked coconut

¾ cup dry sherry, or more as
needed to moisten
granulated sugar for coating

Mix sugar and apricots over low heat to melt sugar. Remove from heat. Work in coconut flakes and sherry to make a firm paste. Roll into balls about ¾ inch in diameter, and then roll in granulated sugar. Store in a covered container and allow to ripen for several weeks.

WEDGEWOOD COVERED BERRY DISH

✳ Date Loaf Sweetmeats

{ Variation of "Apricot Paste," The Experienced
English Housekeeper, *1794 }*

3 cups sugar
1 cup milk
1 pound dates, seeded and chopped

2 cups pecans or walnuts, chopped
⅓ teaspoon salt

Mix sugar and milk and cook to the soft-ball stage (238°). Add dates, nuts and salt, and continue cooking until very thick. Remove from heat and beat until creamy. Shape rolls 1½ to 2 inches in diameter in a wet cloth. Refrigerate until quite cold, or overnight. Cut into slices to serve. *Makes 3 dozen.*

✳ Rum-Chocolate Sweetmeats

2½ cups vanilla-wafer crumbs
1 cup confectioners' sugar
3 tablespoons white corn syrup
⅓ cup rum

2 tablespoons cocoa powder
1 cup pecans or walnuts, chopped
fine

Mix all ingredients together well to form a firm paste, adding more rum to thin if necessary. Roll into ½-inch balls, and dust with additional confectioners' sugar. Store in covered container to ripen for 2 to 3 weeks. These keep well. *Makes 3 dozen.*

✳ Pralines

{ Adapted from "Miss Griffin's Receipt for Caromels,"
Grosvenor, *1850 }*

1 cup granulated sugar
½ cup brown sugar
¼ cup milk

1 tablespoon butter
1 cup pecans
1 teaspoon vanilla extract

Mix all ingredients except vanilla. Bring to a boil and boil for exactly 1½ minutes. Remove from heat, add vanilla, and beat until smooth and creamy. Drop by spoonfuls onto wax paper. *Makes 2 to 3 dozen.*

AMERICAN SILVER SUGAR BOWL
AND CREAM POT, 1797

✳ Candied Orange Peel

{ Adapted from "To Candy Lemon or Orange Peel,"
The Experienced English Housekeeper, *1794 }*

Use 3 large thick-skinned oranges. Remove peel and cut into long narrow strips. Cover peel with cold water and boil for 30 minutes, or until tender. Drain. Cover with cold water and heat to boiling. Repeat this three times, draining well the last time. Pour 1½ cups light corn syrup over peel and cook very slowly until peel is translucent. Remove each piece and allow excess syrup to drain. Roll in granulated sugar and let dry. *Makes about 1 pound.*

✳ Turkish Delight

4 cups granulated sugar
1½ cups water
2 envelopes unflavored gelatin
juice of 1 orange
juice of 1 lemon

grated rind of 1 orange
2 ounces bourbon whiskey
¾ cup chopped pecans
¾ cup shaved almonds
1 cup confectioners' sugar

Combine granulated sugar and 1 cup water in a large kettle and heat to boiling. Soften gelatin in ½ cup water and add to syrup. Simmer for about 20 minutes. Remove from heat and add all other ingredients except confectioners' sugar. Pour into a flat glass pan large enough so that the layer of candy is from ½ to 1 inch deep. Chill until firm. When cold and firm, cut into cubes and roll in confectioners' sugar. Store in refrigerator.

Orange-flower water or rosewater are traditionally used in this Middle East treat. If so desired, substitute ½ cup water for citrus juices, add either flavoring to taste, and green or red food coloring. Chill and roll in confectioners' sugar as above. *Makes about 4 dozen.*

✳ Minted Nuts

1 cup sugar
½ cup water
1 tablespoon light corn syrup
½ teaspoon salt
6 large marshmallows

½ teaspoon peppermint extract, or
3 drops oil of peppermint
3 cups nuts: pecans, almonds or
walnuts

Cook sugar, water, corn syrup and salt together over medium heat to 230° on candy thermometer, or before mixture forms a soft ball. Remove from heat and add marshmallows. Stir until they have melted. Add peppermint and nuts, and stir in a circular motion until nuts are covered and mixture begins to harden. Spread on ungreased paper to cool.

VARIATIONS
1 Colonials also liked to candy raisins in this fashion, but do leave out the peppermint flavoring for fruit. A favorite flavoring was orange-flower water. Add about 1 tablespoon to the syrup if you like.
2 For lime or lemon-glazed walnuts substitute 3 "sprays" of lemon or lime oil spray for peppermint flavoring.

ENGLISH IRON HOT WATER KETTLE
WITH BRASS SPOUT

Bibliography

Booth, Sally Smith, *Hung, Strung and Potted*, Clarkson N. Potter, Inc., New York, 1971.

Brett, Gerard, *Dinner is Served, A Study in Manners*, Archon Books, Hamden, Connecticut, 1969.

Brown, Alice Cooke, *Early American Herb Recipes*, Bonanza Books, Crown Publishers, New York, 1966.

Byrd, William, *The Secret Diary of William Byrd of Westover 1709-1712*, edited by Louis B. Wright and Marion Tinling, Dietz Press, Richmond, Virginia, 1941.

————, *Another Secret Diary of William Byrd of Westover 1739-1741*, edited by Maude H. Woodfin, translated and collated by Marion Tinling, Dietz Press, Richmond, Virginia, 1942.

Carse, Robert, *Ports of Call*, Charles Scribner's Sons, New York, 1967.

Carson, Jane, *Colonial Virginia Cookery*, University Press of Virginia, Charlottesville, Virginia, 1968.

Cavanaugh, J. Albert, *Stencils and Lettering*, privately printed.

Child, Mrs. (L.M.F.), *The American Frugal Housewife*, facsimile edition of the 20th (1836) edition (first publication, Boston, 1829), Harper & Row, New York, 1972.

Ehrenberg, Herman, *With Milam and Fannin, Adventures of a German Boy in Texas' Revolution*, translated by Charlotte Churchill, The Pemberton Press, Austin, Texas, 1968.

Fithian, Philip Vickers, *The Journal and Letters of Philip Vickers Fithian, 1773-1774, A Plantation Tutor of the Old Dominion*, Colonial Williamsburg, Inc., Williamsburg, Virginia, 1965.

Furnas, J. C., *The Americans, A Social History of the United States, 1587-1914*, G. P. Putnam's Sons, New York, 1969.

Glasse, Hannah, *The Art of Cookery Made Plain and Easy*, facsimile edition of 1796 edition published in London, Archon Books, Hamden, Connecticut, and S. R. Publishers, Wakefield, Yorkshire, 1971.

Grosvenor, Rosa Anne Mason (1817-1872), *My Mother's Cookbook*, unpublished, hand-written recipes, about 1850; ms. owned by author's great-granddaughter, Rosa Ann Grosvenor Touret of Providence, Rhode Island.

Hamilton, Doctor Alexander, *Hamilton's Itinerarium; being a Narrative of a Journey*, etc., 1744, edited by Albert Bushnell Hart, privately printed, W. K. Bixby, Saint Louis, Missouri, 1907.

Harrison, Molly H., *The Kitchen in History*, Charles Scribner's Sons, New York, and Osprey Publishers Ltd., Reading, England, 1972.

Hart, Albert Bushnell, and Chapman, A. B., selectors and annotators, *How Our Grandfathers Lived*, The MacMillan Company, New York, 1928.

Hart, Katherine, annotator, *Pease Porridge Hot* (A Waterloo Book for the Friends of the Austin Library), The Encino Press, Austin, Texas, 1967.

Henderson, William Augustus, *The Housekeeper's Instructor or Universal Family Cook*, 9th edition, printed and sold by J. Stratford, London, about 1798.

Janvier, Emma Newbold (1811-1870), *Journal*, Philadelphia, about 1850, unpublished.

King, Rachel Louise, *Receipts*, Brooklyn Heights, New York, about 1870, unpublished.

Krythe, Maymie R., *All About Christmas*, Harper & Brothers, New York, 1954.

Leslie, Miss, *Directions for Cookery, in its Various Branches*, 6th edition, E. L. Carey and A. Hart, Philadelphia, 1839.

————, *Seventy-Five Receipts for Pastry, Cakes, and Sweetmeats*, 10th edition, Munroe and Francis, and Joseph H. Francis, Boston, and Charles S. Francis, New York, 1838.

Loman, Al, compiler and editor, *This Bitterly Beautiful Land—A Texas Commonplace Book*, Roger Beachman, Austin, Texas, 1972.

McKendry, Maxine, *Seven Centuries of English Cooking*, Weidenfeld & Nicolson, Ltd, London, 1973; *The Seven Centuries Cookbook, from Richard II to Elizabeth II*, edited by Arabella Boxer, McGraw-Hill Book Co. Inc., New York, 1973.

Morison, Samuel Eliot, *The Oxford History of the American People*, Oxford University Press, New York, 1965.

New System of Domestic Cookery, Formed upon Principles of Economy and adapted to the Use of Private Families, 2nd edition, Andrews and Cummings, and L. Blake, Boston, 1807.

Olmsted, Frederick Law, *Journey Through Texas in 1853-1854, A Saddle Trip on the Southwestern Frontier*, edited by James Howard, Von Broeckmann-Jones Press, Austin, Texas, 1962.

Phipps, Frances, *Colonial Kitchens, Their Furnishings, and Their Gardens*, Hawthorn Books, Inc., New York, 1972.

Picton, Lida G. Means (Mrs. Charles T. Picton), *Diary*, Alabama, about 1825, unpublished.

The Practical Housewife: A Complete Encyclopaedia of Domestic Economy and Family Medical Guide, J. B. Lippincott Company, Philadelphia, about 1860.

Raffald, Elizabeth, *The Experienced English Housekeeper*, London, 1794.

Randolph, Mrs. Mary, *The Virginia Housewife: or, Methodical Cook*, Hurst & Co., New York, about 1824.

Rice, H.C., and Brown, A.S.K., editors and translators, *The American Campaigns of Rochambeau's Army*, Princeton University Press, Princeton, New Jersey, and Brown University Press, Providence, Rhode Island, 1972.

Roberts, Patricia Easterbrook, *Table Settings, Entertaining, and Etiquette, A History and Guide*, Thames and Hudson, Ltd., London, and Bonanza Books, Crown Publishers, New York, 1967.

Simmons, Amelia, *American Cookery; or, The Art of Dressing Viands, Fish, Poultry & Vegetables; and the best Modes of Making Pastes, Puffs, Pies, Tarts, Puddings, Custards & Preserves*, etc., facsimile edition of the original 1796 edition, Wm. B. Eerdmans Publishing Company, Grand Rapids, Michigan, 1965.

Smith, E., *The Compleat Housewife: or, Accomplish'd Gentlewoman's Companion*, 12th edition, J. and H. Pemberton, London, 1744.

Spry, Constance, and Hume, Rosemary, *The Constance Spry Cookery Book*, J. M. Dent & Sons, Ltd., London, 1967.

Stuyvesant, Jared, "Christmas Cakes and Ale," *Country Life Magazine*, December, 1907.

Touret, Rosa Ann Grosvenor, *An American Family in the Nineteenth Century*, privately printed, 1973. (*see also* Grosvenor)

Treman, Elizabeth Lovejoy (Mrs. Mynderse Van Cleef), *Treasured Family Recipes from Three Generations*, Ithaca, New York, late nineteenth century, unpublished.

The Vintner's, Brewer's, Spirit Merchant's and Licensed Victuller's Guide, by "A Practical Man," 4th edition, Charles Frederick Cock, London, 1829.

Waring, Janet, *Early American Stencils on Walls and Furniture*, Dover Publications, Inc., New York, 1968.

Warren, Phelps, *Irish Glass*, Charles Scribner's Sons, New York, and Faber & Faber, London, 1970.

Wertenbaker, Thomas J., *The Golden Age of Colonial Culture*, Great Seal Books, Cornell University Press, Ithaca, New York, 1963.

Wright, Louis B., *The Cultural Life of the American Colonies*, Harper & Brothers, New York, 1957.

Glossary

à la russe: nineteenth-century French fashion of having servants present dishes of food to diners seated at table.

ashcakes: a simple bread made from cornmeal, grease and water, wrapped in cabbage leaves, and cooked among smoldering fireplace logs.

bevridge: forerunner of modern cola drink, made from spring water, molasses and ginger.

bumper: a cup or glass filled to the brim, especially for a toast.

cast and scour: vomit.

caudle: hot custardlike wine drink.

cimblins: white or pale green flat squash with scalloped edges.

comfit: a sweetmeat made of sugared roots and seeds.

dainties: secondary desserts such as fresh fruits, macaroons, sugared raisins, sweet relishes, quinces.

firing glass: or hammering glass, heavy-footed, used to thump on the table as a form of acclamation.

flummery: jellied dessert of cream, wine.

fool: a sweet, creamy custard served cold.

gammon: ham.

hardtack: a kind of bread, baked to very hard consistency, similar to today's Norwegian flatbread.

hoecakes: a simple bread made of meal and water cooked on a hoe blade over fire, like a pancake.

jerky: meat cut in thin strips dried in the sun by Indians, to make a hard dried preserved meat. Colonists later dried the meat in smokehouses.

johnnycakes: similar to hoecakes, pancakes made of cornmeal and cooked until quite crusty outside and soft inside.

lug poles: wood or iron poles in fireplace wall providing rack for hanging cooking pots over fire.

made dish: a dish that included several ingredients and took more time to prepare, such as a stew or ragoo.

metheglin: drink of wine, honey and herbs.

noggin': pottery or wooden pitcher passed as communal bowl to drink from, used in taverns.

pasties: stuffed small pastries.

pastry jigger: utensil used to decorate cookie edges.

pearlash: potassium carbonate; potash mixed with other salts.

pease: early word for peas.

peel: long-handled wooden paddle for removing bread from oven.

pie crimper: utensil to press edges of pastry against pie pan before cooking.

posset: hot drink of milk, ale, spices and bread crumbs.

potash: the alkaline remains from burning certain vegetables or wood ashes in iron pots.

potted: food packed into earthenware container and sealed with clarified butter (for example, Potted Cheese).

rasping: scraping burnt crust from freshly baked bread.

receipts: early word for recipes.

removes: dishes removed from the dining table during a course and replaced with others; for example, a large piece of meat replaced by a large fish.

rout: late-evening party featuring dancing, cards and a lavish dessert buffet and drinks and punches.

rye 'n' Injun: Colonial bread of corn and rye meal mixed.

sallat: salad.

scratchbacks: muffins of a thick corn pudding uneven on top, hence they scratched the roof of the mouth when eaten.

sippets: small pieces of toast fried in butter.

smokejack: air-driven jack. When placed over fire in a fireplace, the updraft causes it to function.

sousing: method of fancy pickling.

standing salt: large saltcellar.

suckets: candied peels and dried sweetmeats.

sucket spoon: eating utensil with fork on one end and spoon on the other.

sweetmeats: small bite-sized sweets, such as sugared fruits and nuts, candied rose petals and violets.

switchel: a drink of molasses, ginger, vinegar and rum, enjoyed by sailors.

syllabub: a dessert of cream or milk, lemon and wine.

treenware: wooden ware, an English term; word derived from the word "tree." During early times when glass, silver and china were restricted to the wealthy, small articles were made of wood, such as spoons, bowls, mugs and trenchers.

trencher: the earliest form of plate, an English term; earliest ones were made of thick slices of bread. Wooden trenchers had a depression carved in the center.

voiders: large baskets used to put dishes in when removing them from the dining table.

wine rinsers: also called wineglass coolers, monteiths, or finger bowls. Introduced to America in the eighteenth century. Rinsers had one or two lips in the rim. Large bowls with scalloped edges for 6 to 8 glasses were called monteiths and were also used as punch bowls.

wine slides: or wine coasters, circular stands for bottles or decanters for table use. Usually silver slides with wood bases. Introduced in mideighteenth century in pairs, sets of four, or more.

Index

Index

Index

Index

179